# BREAKING BREAD

# BREAKING BREAD

## The Spiritual Significance of Food

SARA COVIN JUENGST

WESTMINSTER/JOHN KNOX PRESS
Louisville, Kentucky

*Book design by Publishers' WorkGroup*

*First edition*

This book is printed on acid-free paper that meets the American National Standards Institute Z39.48 standard.

Published by Westminster/John Knox Press
Louisville, Kentucky

PRINTED IN THE UNITED STATES OF AMERICA

9   8   7   6   5   4   3   2

**Library of Congress Cataloging-in-Publication Data**

Juengst, Sara Covin.
    Breaking bread : the spiritual significance of food / Sara Covin Juengst. — 1st ed.
            p.      cm.
    Includes bibliographical references.
    ISBN 0-664-25383-0

    1. Food in the Bible.   2. Food—Religious aspects—Christianity.
3. Table—Religious aspects—Christianity.    4. Fasts and feasts in the Bible.    5. Fasts and feasts.    I. Title.
BS680.F6J84 1992
220.8'6413—dc20                                                91-38151

*This book is dedicated to my family who have experienced
the bonding power of the table in the midst of change*

---

# CONTENTS

# FOREWORD

Sara Juengst's new book, *Breaking Bread,* offers us fresh insight into the real meaning of those lovely words "bread of life." With knowledge and grace the author explores a topic—food—that many of us would relegate to the ho-hum realm of daily maintenance or to the rarefied realm of the special occasion; she shows us instead how food is woven as intricately as faith into the entire fabric of our lives. She has written not a cookbook but a book of days, which reveals how food is served—and serves us—at moments of joy and suffering, work and play, solitude and community, life and death. If ever there was a book that could honestly be described as "food for thought," this is it.

I am one of those people, sad to tell, who has regarded food primarily as fuel. Though I enjoy a good meal and would rather have something simple and wholesome than the stuff they hand me through the car window, I have been largely insensitive to the symbolic meanings of eating, to the ways eating is and always has been a dimension of depth in the human story. But now, thanks to Sara Juengst, I have a new way of understanding what it means to eat together and alone.

As a Christian, I should have come to this understanding earlier. As *Breaking Bread* so richly demonstrates, the biblical texts of my own tradition are laden with stories of food and eating—and, more often than not, these stories overflow with meaning.

Think, for example, of the biblical story from which the book's title is taken. Jesus has been crucified, and the disciples are walking home along the road to Emmaus, downcast and defeated and in despair. A stranger joins them and asks why they are so forlorn. They ridicule him for not knowing what is going on (a bit of ironic humor, as the story turns out!) and explain to him that their leader, their hope, is dead and gone. The stranger berates them for their faithlessness, for not recalling the promises of the prophets, but the disciples will have none of it. Then, realizing it is getting late, they offer the hospitality that was ordinary in their world but is becoming extraordinary in ours: They invite the stranger to their home for a bite to eat.

That is when it happens, at table. That is when the disciples first understand that resurrection is more real than death. That is when they learn the truth that will overturn their world and ours: The stranger is the risen Christ, "and he was known to them in the breaking of bread."

Sara Juengst knows that the meal shared with Jesus by the Emmaus-bound disciples is not a one-of-a-kind event, frozen in time and space as a religious artifact or antiquity. It is a meal that has been served many times since, if only we have eyes to see. As I reread the Emmaus story through Sara Juengst's eyes, I wonder how often I have been able to touch something of the Christ-life in the breaking of bread. The answer is: frequently—in fact, I am astonished at the number of such memories I have.

I have understood my love for other people across the table, and I have known their love for me. At mealtimes I have confessed offenses against people I care for, and I have received their forgiveness as well. I have deepened my sense of calling in late-night conversations sustained by snacks, and in sunlit rooms at breakfast I have felt the renewal of energy to pursue that calling in spite of the obstacles. In many times and places, I have experienced the Christ-life in the breaking of bread.

None of this will surprise Sara Juengst, because she has long understood the spirituality of eating and feeding. From her rich experience as cook and hostess and theologian and teacher, she has given us a book that nourishes us on many levels—intellectually, spiritually, and in the common practices of our daily lives. I am grateful for the meal she has put before us, and for her warm welcome to this table. I know that you will be too. Sit, eat, and *bon appetit!*

*Parker J. Palmer*

# PREFACE

During the ten years that my husband and I taught in the Republic of Zaire, we learned much from our African friends about the true meaning of hospitality. There was always room for one more around the African cooking pot. As we were invited to sit around that pot and, in the African idiom, "put our feet in the fire" with our African friends, we understood in a new way the bonding power of food. In those years, entertaining friends became not only our chief recreation but a way to build friendships across racial, national, and cultural barriers. I kept a diary of guest meals so that I would not repeat the Beef Stroganoff every time the Reilys, the Wakutekas, or the Van Overbeeks came to visit. Today, as I look at the names of those persons who sat to eat with us—friends not only from Zaire but from France, Haiti, the Netherlands, Italy, Belgium, Canada, Zambia, Finland, and other places—I realize that we were experiencing a very special bonding around our table. Friendships became richer and deeper in the act of breaking bread together.

We also learned about the connection of food and compassion during times of severe drought, famine, and tribal war in Africa. We were deeply moved to be a part of the efforts of the Christian church to carry out the "Inasmuch" of the Gospel message, distributing rice, flour, oil, and dried beans supplied by ordinary Christians from around the world to folk in desperate need of "daily bread."

And celebration! Feasts accompany every important occasion in Africa:

baptisms, graduations, rites of passage, the choice of a village chief, weddings, funerals. Our African friends understood how food has the power both to comfort and console and to gladden the heart. Although it was usually the fatted goat, not the calf, that was killed on joyous occasions, I understood the parable of the lost son much better after being a part of these celebrations.

Thirty-seven years ago, one of my wedding presents was *The Betty Crocker Picture Cookbook.* It set my imagination on fire. I vowed to try every single recipe, even though at the time I was not sure how to boil an egg. As I experimented with Pompano en Papillote and Chicken Cacciatore, I experienced the thrill of discovering the incredible variety of food from around the world and the satisfaction of sharing that discovery with others.

In the years since then, as a minister and educator, I have become fascinated by food and feasting in the Bible. Careful exegesis of biblical passages about food has opened my eyes to the metaphorical and liturgical significance of food in the Old and New Testaments. Understanding the biblical customs connected with food has enabled me to discover new meaning in familiar passages. I have combined some of these insights here in a study of six theological themes related to food and feasting.

These chapters are designed to serve as a tool for serious study of an important biblical symbol. Once again I have the satisfaction of sharing my discoveries about food with others, this time without setting a table. I hope this book will be as exciting to eager students of the Bible as Betty Crocker's cookbook was to a new bride, and that the results of reading it will be as nourishing.

# 1    BIBLICAL FOODS AND CUSTOMS

Most people eat as if they were fattening themselves for market.
—Edgar Watson Howe

"What's for lunch?"
"Soup's on!"
"How about a cup of coffee?"
"Are you coming for dinner?"
"Potluck supper at church Wednesday night!"
"Let's eat!"

Familiar words in most households. Gathering together to eat has been a central part of both family and community life since families and communities began.

Eating together involves more than just appeasing hunger. It is an activity that includes sharing, celebration, learning from one another, and providing for the helpless, a ritual that brings comfort, satisfaction, pleasure, creativity, sustenance, nurture, appreciation, and healing. It satisfies many levels of human needs.

According to Abraham Maslow's famous hierarchy, it is only when basic needs are supplied that others can be met. One of those basic needs is nourishment to sustain life. After that need is met, the dimensions of aesthetics, pleasure, ritual, and celebration come into play.

Eating together is a circular action. Whether the family that once circled the campfire has taken chairs around a rectangular linen-clad table with silver candelabra and an elegantly arranged centerpiece, or just sat down at a rough picnic table, the mood is still circular: a gathering around the festal board where food is spread to be shared.

The sharing of food has the special symbolic significance of breaking down barriers, getting to know people, demonstrating oneness. Church suppers, business lunches, family reunions, alumni banquets: all revolve around food.

One of the characteristics of the technological society, however, has been a loosening of the bonds of the table. Short-order restaurants, frozen foods, hectic and varied family schedules, even microwave ovens have all contributed to the shrinking of the rituals of food preparation and eating together. In the 1960 movie *The Apartment*, Jack Lemmon provided an unforgettable image of the lonely bachelor popping a TV dinner into the stove and sitting at his coffee table to consume it right from its aluminum pan.

As a humorist on National Public Radio said ruefully about the proliferation of fancy cookbooks, "Everybody buys them, but nobody has time to cook anymore." The very conveniences that are supposed to make meal preparation easier seem to rob cooking of the loving, careful preparation that made the final outcome so glorious. The smell of onions on the chopping board and soup simmering on the back of the stove has been replaced by the instant magic of the microwave or the frozen dinner—or by the all too familiar "Let's eat out, I don't feel like cooking!"

A sociologist recently noted that the marriages of couples who eat breakfast together seem to last longer. Unfortunately, the family breakfast has almost totally disappeared in most American homes. Television commercials routinely show family members dashing through the kitchen at breakfast time on the way to school or work, while the mother desperately urges them to "eat something!"

Whatever happened to the family togetherness of breakfast in the dining room, with a properly set table? With a prayer to start the busy day ahead? With a sharing of plans for the day? With a taking notice of one another?

### BIBLICAL FEASTS

Feasting is clearly of central importance in the Bible. There are "appointed feasts"—set times and occasions when the community gathered to eat and worship together—and many informal times of eating and drinking that are central to the unfolding of the biblical narrative. Later chapters will consider Isaiah's description of a great picnic on the mountain, the gathering of the twelve with their teacher in an upper room, the importance of invitations to banquet tables. Meals are used for teaching (Jesus' eating with outcasts) and to demonstrate compassion (feeding the multitudes). The very word "covenant" may be derived from the Hebrew word meaning "to eat with salt."

In the Old Testament, the word "feast," *ḥag* (Haggai means "born on a feast day"), usually referred to the three great pilgrim festivals: Unleavened Bread, Weeks, and Booths. These were not sober, dignified, solemn feasts. They included processions, dancing, feasting, and sometimes drunkenness. The verb is translated in Psalm 107:27 as "reeled" and reminds us of the graphic picture of "feasting" that took place at the golden calf.

At the heart of the Old Testament pilgrim feasts were the festal sacrifices. These were

> mainly communal meals, eaten with great joy. The eating of meat, a relatively rare occurrence in ancient Israel, and originally always having a religious significance, coupled with the drinking of wine, gave to a feast both its festal and its sacral character. . . . God himself was assumed to participate symbolically by receiving the choice portions of fat which were burned on the altar. . . . As has been emphasized in recent scholarship, the great feasts were occasions of "covenant renewal" at which the bonds that held Israel together as the people of God were reknit.[1]

Besides these great pilgrim festivals, there are other kinds of feasts in the Bible: banquets, suppers, and impromptu picnics and family meals. Some of the foods used in biblical times are still familiar to us today, while others, such as manna and locusts, are not part of our daily diet. We have already noted that meat was reserved primarily for ritual or highly celebrative occasions. The fatted calf of the lost son parable (Luke 15) and the roasted lamb of the Passover Supper are among the most well-known menus of the Bible. "Bring on the fatted calf" has entered our language as an expression of extravagant welcome.

Of course, there were exceptions. Solomon's splendor is evident in the list of household food items for one day (1 Kings 4:22–23): ten fat oxen and one hundred sheep, besides deer, gazelles, roebucks, and fatted fowl, to say nothing of thirty measures of fine flour and threescore measures of meal. Another lavish meat dinner occurred when Elisha received Elijah's mantle (1 Kings 19:19–21). Before answering the call to become Elijah's successor, Elisha returned home and killed a yoke of oxen, boiled them, and gave them to the people as a magnificent farewell gesture.

EVERYDAY MEALS

For most people in biblical times, however, meals were very simple. Fish was an important part of the diet of the people of the Holy Land. The disciples were having a fish breakfast on the beach when Jesus appeared to them after his resurrection (John 21). Often the fish were cooked in milk and served with cheese, or cooked with leeks, or eaten with eggs. Some were salted, dried, or pickled. There were three main types: tilapia, carp, and catfish. The importance of fish in the lives of the people made it an important symbol, which Jesus used often in his teaching. Later, of course, because of the anagram of the Greek word for fish, *ichthys*, it became a symbol for "Jesus Christ" or "Christian."

What about chicken? Although no mention is made of the Colonel's secret recipe in the scriptures, various kinds of fowl do appear. Solomon distributed fatted fowl to his household, and the children of Israel ate quail in the desert. Since the words "cock" and "goose" do not appear in the Old Testament, it is reasonable to assume that the Hebrews did not raise domesticated fowl, at least in the period of the monarchy, so the ones on Solomon's table were probably game birds. Since some seals from the Babylonian period have cocks on them, it is reasonable to assume that the fowls prepared for Nehemiah (Neh. 5:18) were game, pigeons, or possibly domestic fowl.[2] Eggs are mentioned in the Old Testament but were probably from wild birds (Deut. 22:6 and Isa. 10:14). Jesus spoke of wanting to protect Jerusalem as a hen does her chickens, and Peter's denials were punctuated by a cock crowing, so it seems evident that domesticated fowl were well known in Jesus' day. Perhaps Martha was preparing a chicken dinner for Jesus that memorable day he visited in her home.

Vegetables, fruits, and herbs were also an important part of the Hebrew diet. Among those mentioned are corn (wheat or millet), lentils, leeks, onions, garlic, cucumbers, beans, pomegranates, grapes, mint, cinnamon, cumin, rue, dill, mustard, bitter herbs, dates, olives, figs, almonds, and apples (although what is meant by "apple" may in reality have been citron or quince). Many of these foods were used as images in the teaching of the prophets and of Jesus. In addition to these vegetarian items, the diet included milk, cheese, curds, salt, wild honey, oil, and wine. Sirach lists the necessities of life as "salt, wheat, milk, honey, wine, and oil" (Ecclus. 39:26).

A staple of the diet was cereal: barley and emmer (a sort of wheat), made into bread (Ruth 2); millet and spelt, sometimes eaten fresh or roasted.[3] Elisha ate "fresh ears of grain" uncooked (2 Kings 4:42–44). The king himself ate the heads of grain roasted or parched in a pan (1 Sam. 25:18). Perhaps these were the "ears of grain" Jesus' disciples picked as they walked through the fields (Mark 2:23), which provided an occasion for teaching about the true meaning of the law.

In many other places in the Bible, food is mentioned both literally and figuratively. In the Sermon on the Mount, Jesus spoke of salt and fruit and bread and of not worrying about having enough food and drink to stay alive. In his parables, he used the images of yeast, wedding feasts, and banquet tables, and in his teaching he reminded his hearers often of the importance of feeding the hungry. The book of Revelation speaks of the happiness of those who are invited to "the wedding feast" (19:9, TEV).

But what does all this have to do with us? What can ancient rituals of feasting teach us about how to live richer and more fruitful lives?

In *A Concise Encyclopaedia of Gastronomy*, André Simon writes, "Bread, Wine, and Oil, that blessed trinity of the kindly fruits of the earth, have been, ever since biblical times, the symbol of peace—and plenty, the reward promised by angels in heaven to those of goodwill upon earth."[4] A full belly is a blessing indeed.

But the scriptures also offer a word of caution to all of us who risk being "overfed," who live in a land where obesity is the nation's largest health problem. It is found in the prayer in Proverbs 30:8–9 (TEV): "Give me only as much food as I need. If I have more, I might say I do not need you."

Food: a blessed gift indeed but, like all good gifts, one that risks abuse. How can we celebrate the gift of food in ways that glorify the Giver? How can we use mealtimes to strengthen our bonds with those we meet, both family and strangers? How can we use food to enrich and enlarge our worship, our play, our health, our compassion?

The task of this book is to show how the scriptures provide clues for nourishing our hungry lives, to encourage reexamination of our use of food, and to provide practical suggestions for making the breaking of bread a celebrative, bonding, compassionate ritual in our contemporary lives.

# 2      STEWARDSHIP

## *Food as God's Good Gift*

What God gives and what we take,
'Tis a gift for Christ His sake:
Be the meal of beans and pease,
God be thanked for those and these:
Have we flesh, or have we fish,
All are fragments from his dish.
        —Robert Herrick

Blessed art Thou,
O Lord our God,
king of the world,
who bringest forth bread from the earth.
        —Ancient Jewish blessing

The poem by Herrick and the beautiful prayer repeated in Jewish homes for thousands of years echo a theme that occurs again and again in the Bible: "Every perfect gift is from above" (James 1:17).

It seems so obvious . . . but we forget. Even while we are praying, "Give us this day our daily bread," we are worrying about whether we will be able to pay for this week's groceries or what the menu should be for Friday's guests. The basic biblical affirmation about food is that God is the giver of our daily bread. Psalm 104 is beautifully specific:

> From the sky you send rain on the hills,
>     and the earth is filled with your blessings.
> You make grass grow for the cattle
>     and plants for man to use
> so that he can grow his crops
>     and produce wine to make him happy,
>     olive oil to make him cheerful,
>     and bread to give him strength.
> Psalm 104:13–15, TEV

The point is clear. God is the source of the nourishment that sustains our lives. The psalmist goes on to say (vs. 27–28, RSV)

> These all look to thee,
>     to give them their food in due season.
> When thou givest to them, they gather it up;
>     when thou openest thy hand, they are filled with good things.

## GOD AS GARDENER

The promise of food was an integral part of the covenant God made with the Israelites:

> If you live according to my laws and obey my commands, I will send you rain at the right time, so that the land will produce crops and the trees will bear fruit. Your crops will be so plentiful that you will still be harvesting grain when it is time to pick grapes, and you will still be picking grapes when it is time to plant grain. You will have all that you want to eat, and you can live in safety in your land.
> —Leviticus 26:3–5, TEV

For a nomadic people, this sounded like a description of paradise.

The writer of Ecclesiastes makes an emphatic claim: "All of us should eat and drink and enjoy what we have worked for. It is God's gift" (Eccl. 3:13, TEV). This was a logical connection for the Israelites to make. They believed in a Creator God who not only made the universe but cared enough about it to continue to sustain it. The Creation story affirms that from the beginning God provided for human needs by planting a garden for food.

> And God said, "Behold, I have given you every plant yielding seed which is upon the face of all the earth, and every tree with seed in its fruit; you shall have them for food. . . . " And God saw everything that he had made, and behold, it was very good.
>
> —Genesis 1:29, 31

This care has never ceased. God's creation was not complete without a cycle of sustenance, a loving, caring arrangement for supplying the basic necessities of life.

The image of God as gardener was one that appealed to the Israelites. It was not unusual for them to speak of God's activity in terms of their own daily routines. The description of the Promised Land centered around the vision of a wonderful garden, overflowing not only with the familiar milk and honey but with an abundance of other good things. The description in Deuteronomy 8 reads like a real estate brochure aimed at would-be farmers:

> For the LORD your God is bringing you into a good land, a land of brooks of water, of fountains and springs, flowing forth in valleys and hills, a land of wheat and barley, of vines and fig trees and pomegranates, a land of olive trees and honey, a land in which you will eat bread without scarcity, in which you will lack nothing, a land whose stones are iron, and out of whose hills you can dig copper. And you shall eat and be full, and you shall bless the LORD your God for the good land he has given you.
>
> —Deuteronomy 8:7–10

This good land, prepared by God the gardener, became a symbol for the Israelites of God's care for them. It was the answer to prayer for a group of wanderers who for forty years had been carving out a meager existence in a barren wilderness. The vision of its richness and fullness kept them going through those difficult days. They had been given a land in which they would always have bread. The covenant promise had taken on the reality of wheat and pomegranates, and as they broke bread they would remember in gratitude the One who had provided it.

The image of God as gardener appears in Isaiah 28:23–29 in parable form. This parable gives us the picture of a God who not only patiently instructs farmers in agricultural methods but who acts in purposeful, orderly ways just as a farmer does. Isaiah is reminding the people that life is not chaotic and meaningless. We have not been abandoned by our God and left to drift through space unguided, uncared for, by a heartless creator. Instead, creation was just the beginning of God's provision for us; God's hand continues to water and nourish us, even in the most difficult times.

Walter Brueggemann speaks of the need to make visible links between the "overpowering miracle of creation" and the "daily reality of food." We do this at the table when we pray, "Bless this food." It is in the table grace, Brueggemann says, that we acknowledge that we "live by grace and know that we are strangely sustained, nurtured, and nourished."[1] The covenant promise is that God is constantly working with all the loving patience of a good gardener to supply our needs.

While the theme of God as the giver of food is not reiterated as often in the New Testament as in the Old, it is clearly there. Matthew reminds us in the Sermon on the Mount (6:31–33):

> Therefore do not be anxious, saying, "What shall we eat?" or "What shall we drink?" or "What shall we wear?" For the Gentiles seek all these things; and your heavenly Father knows that you need them all. But seek first his kingdom and his righteousness, and all these things shall be yours as well.

Søren Kierkegaard said about this passage that Jesus in no way suggests that our lives would be more Christian if we did without food, drink, clothing, and other sources of pleasure and satisfaction, but that these things can be good if they support our relationship to God rather than compete with it. When we recognize that all these good things are gifts, then we live in trust that God will supply what we need. That trust gives us confidence and removes our anxiety. The image is one of startling simplicity: gift + trust = confidence . . . confidence like that of a child who does not question, but simply assumes that the daily bread will be there. This attitude of trust molds behavior.[2]

Jesus underlined this confidence when he taught his disciples to pray, "Give us this day our daily bread" (Matt. 6:11). He took physical needs seriously throughout his life. Although scholars do not agree as to whether the word "daily" means "necessary" or "today's" or "for the coming day," it is clear that the petition reminds us that we may lie down to sleep without despair, knowing that God will provide for the coming day.

And yet there is a tension. Even while relying on God's providential care, we must not simply fold our hands and do nothing, saying smugly, "The Lord will provide." Douglas John Hall, in his excellent book *Imaging God*, speaks of the tension between God's authority and our responsibility but says it is possible to live within it, believing both in "the entire indispensability of grace and the absolute necessity of the most mature human thought, word, and deed."[3] This maturity is reflected in the poor who live without despair, but in hope; and in the rich who live without greed and hoarding, but in love.

The image of God as gardener appears frequently in Jesus' parables. The word "sow" was frequently used by rabbis as a metaphor for teaching, so it was natural for Jesus to use this image for God as "sower" or teacher.

Although Jesus' parables celebrate the miracle of growth, the emphasis is not on the growth of crops but on the growth of righteousness. But the same God who gives food to the hungry (Ps. 146:7) feeds those who "hunger and thirst for righteousness" (Matt. 5:6). Two of these gardening parables are:

> The parable of the mustard seed (Luke 13:18–19): The seed of the kingdom has been planted by God, and no one can destroy it.
>
> The parable of the sower (Luke 8:11–15): When the gospel is preached faithfully, God will bring in the harvest.

Matthew used the metaphor of God as gardener when he described Jesus' response to the Pharisees' anger over his teachings. Jesus' answer was, "Every plant which my heavenly Father has not planted will be rooted up" (Matt. 15:13).

In all these passages the familiar Old Testament image of God as the loving gardener who provides food has been transformed into the image of the God who is still planting seed and who will bring in the rich harvest of the kingdom, a Creator who cares and who will provide the "wine and milk without money and without price" of which the prophet Isaiah spoke (55:1).

## BREAD AND LAUGHTER

The words of Psalm 104 and Ecclesiastes 3:13 quoted earlier remind us that food meets many needs. It does more than just sustain life. Science fiction has been predicting for years that human beings will soon give up food preparation and resort to an array of multicolored pills, dehydrated foods, and vitamin supplements. But, although this is theoretically possible, we have not yet given up the succulent aromas and textures of sautéed onions, broiled beef, and toasted nuts. We eat to satisfy our physical hunger, but we also eat for comfort and for enjoyment. Food is a source of pleasure. The smell of fresh-baked bread, the taste of just-picked corn, the sight of strawberries mounded with snowy cream, the texture of melted cheese on corn chips: all these set our mouths watering.

One Methodist minister, described as "the nation's first food evangelist," who believes in the celebration of food is Jeff Smith, known to millions as TV's Frugal Gourmet. Smith sees the preparation and enjoyment of food as a sacramental ritual that brings fellowship and meaning into a depersonalized age. "I want your family to feast together and be together when they eat," Smith says repeatedly. His message is not new. It is profoundly biblical. We find it in Ecclesiastes: "There is nothing better for a man than that he should eat and drink, and find enjoyment in his toil. This also, I saw, is from the hand of God; for apart from him who can eat or who can have enjoyment?" (Eccl. 2:24–25); "Eat your bread with enjoyment" (Eccl. 9:7); and "Bread is made for laughter" (Eccl. 10:19).

The reverse side of the message is the warning contained in several proverbs about eating without joy: "Better is a dinner of herbs where love is than a fatted ox and hatred with it" (Prov. 15:17), and "Better is a dry morsel with quiet than a house full of feasting with strife" (Prov. 17:1).

No matter how festive the fare, no matter how good the intentions, the scriptural wisdom is true: if the meal is served with bitterness, anger, or resentment, it is a failure. A gourmet menu cannot make up the difference.

Jesus understood about the enjoyment of food. After the tax collector Levi had accepted Jesus' call, "Follow me," Jesus gave a celebrative feast, according to Luke (Luke 5:29–39). The Pharisees were outraged and began criticizing Jesus, not only for eating with sinners but for not following the rigorous, ascetic lifestyle practiced by John the Baptist and his followers, which included much fasting. Fasting, however, was not Jesus' way.

Why did Jesus not adhere strictly to the Jewish laws? The answer is that his message was something so new it could not be expressed in the old forms. The freeing power of Christ shatters old conceptions of righteousness. Jesus used the image of new wineskins, new ways of living: a profound new sense of joy that expressed itself in enjoying food and drink with friends. It was this exuberant enjoyment of God's good gifts that made some people label Jesus "a glutton and a drunkard" (Luke 7:34). In reality, he was restoring to religious life something that had been lost under layers of legalism and rigid asceticism.

The early Christian church modeled this "new wine" lifestyle. "And day by day, attending the temple together and breaking bread in their homes, they partook of food with glad and generous hearts" (Acts 2:46). No pietistic fasting here!

Barnabas and Paul, in trying to prevent the people of Lystra from worshiping them as gods, pointed out to them that it was the "living God" who had given them "rains and fruitful seasons, satisfying your hearts with food and gladness" (Acts 14:17). Food and gladness: in the New Testament, as in the Old, these two words belong together.

Food not only brings joy, it has a mysterious power to bring comfort in moments of despair. Some of the most heart-appealing commercials on TV are about the power of food to soothe and comfort: biting into a tender chocolate chip cookie, sharing a cup of cinnamon-flavored coffee with a friend on a rainy evening, perching on a porch railing to enjoy a crunchy bowl of cereal. These images send us scurrying to find a cure for our own malaise or loneliness or depression in, as Winnie-the-Pooh would say, "a little smackerel of something."

And it's biblical. Not only does Psalm 104 speak of the heart-strengthening power of bread (this is where we get the expression "Bread is the staff of life"), but the Song of Solomon reveals an understanding of the ability of food to comfort and console when the lovesick woman begs (2:5), "Sustain me with raisins, refresh me with apples; for I am sick with love." The "raisins" in this passage were probably the raisin "cakes" mentioned in Hosea 3:1 that were used in fertility cults. We are all familiar with the sweet-tooth craving which comes over us when we are bored or nervous or even in love.

Many of us are also familiar with another way in which food is used to comfort: the custom of bringing food to bereaved families. Not only is this a concrete gesture of love and support at a time of sorrow, but the food itself can relieve anxiety and sadness. One dying mother, recognizing this, arranged for her old housekeeper to fix her grown children's favorite foods, to be ready when they came for her funeral, to remind them of their childhood meals and of the real qualities of home that would live on.

Perhaps the supreme expression of the comfort of food is found in the beloved Twenty-third Psalm: "Thou preparest a table before me in the presence of my enemies; thou anointest my head with oil; my cup overflows" (v. 5). With the poet, we reflect on the meaning of the sacrificial meal in the house of God. As our hearts are filled with joy at being able to take part in the ritual, we are comforted by the realization of how God has honored us. We have been the recipients of God's hospitality, the guests of God who have been fed by God's own hand. The warmth of this knowledge overrides the bitterness of broken human relations. This is the Ultimate Chocolate Chip Cookie! Enjoying God's gift of food becomes a means of grace, enabling us to cope with our sorrows and even with those who reject us.

## FOOD AS SACRAMENT

We have observed that in biblical theology God is the giver, the good gardener who provides food. We have noted how we, who are the recipients of God's gifts, find both joy and comfort in food.

As we read the Bible, however, another layer of meaning surfaces. Food, since it is the gift of God, is to be treated sacramentally. Dictionaries describe "sacramental" as having a sacred character or meaning. In the Old Testament, the sacred character of food is both explicit (as when it is used for sacrifices) and implicit (as in the Leviticus laws governing eating). Its sacredness is evident in its being a part of the covenant promise: the Lord provides food for those who fear him; he is ever mindful of his covenant" (Ps. 111:5).

How do we treat food in a sacramental way? What does the Old Testament say about how food is to be used? How does this apply to us today?

The diversity of good things that come from God's hand is enormous. God has also given the human mind ingenuity, and today that ingenuity has produced such complexity in food that we are baffled and bewildered about how to choose. Almost two centuries ago, Joseph Addison wrote:

> Should we not think a man mad who at one meal will devour fowl, flesh, and fish; swallow oil, and vinegar, salt, wines, and spices; throw down salads of twenty different herbs, sauces of an hundred ingredients, confections and fruits of numberless sweets and flavours? For my part, when I behold a table set out in all its magnificence, I fancy that I see gouts and dropsies, fevers and lethargies, and other innumerable distempers, lying in ambuscade among the dishes.[4]

Perhaps not many of us have ever tasted a sauce of a hundred ingredients, but it is obvious that we no longer exist on the simple diet of biblical times: bread and cheese and wine. We are deluged each year by an avalanche of new cookbooks, new TV cooking shows, and exotic produce from other countries. We are bombarded by information on what to include—or not to include—in our diets. We are haunted by words like cholesterol and fiber and sodium content. We are not sure how to eat wisely or well.

Although the Bible was written before people knew about vitamins and bran and polyunsaturated oils, it does contain an understanding of the relationship between nutrition and the responsible religious life. The dietary laws of Leviticus and Deuteronomy may seem strange to us, but they formed an important part of the religious life of the Israelites.

The seventh chapter of Leviticus says that no fat or blood can be eaten. To break this law meant that one could no longer be considered one of God's people. The reasons for these prohibitions had nothing to do with cholesterol or obesity. Fat was not to be eaten; it was to be used in burnt offerings. Blood was not to be eaten; it contained life, and was therefore sacred. This explicit understanding of the sacred nature of food was integral to the worship of the people.

The necessities of life, according to Sirach, as we saw in the last chapter, were salt, wheat, milk, honey, wine, and oil. With the exception of salt and wine, these sound like the basic staples of a health food store. And yet in spite of this simple diet, there are many biblical warnings about the dangers of gluttony.

The marvelous story of how Daniel and his friends resisted the king's rich food and wine and ate only vegetables and water should warm the hearts of vegetarians. The youths in the Daniel story, however, are not abstaining from the king's food because they believe vegetarianism will prevent disease, but because they are afraid the king's food might contain something that would cause them to become ceremonially defiled. Eating only vegetables and water would prevent that from happening. The story underscores the sacramental importance that food had for the Jews. Breaking one of the dietary laws was as serious as idolatry.

Finally, the Old Testament urges us to keep food in its proper perspective.

Isaiah's invitation to "eat what is good" (Isa. 55:2) reminded the children of Israel that the hunger they felt, even after eating, could not be assuaged by lavish amounts of milk and grain and wine. It reminds us, too, that varied menus and healthy diets cannot fill the emptiness of lives lived outside a covenant relationship with God. "Come, buy wine and milk without money and without price . . . that your soul may live" (Isa. 55:1, 3).

> "May our garners be full,
>     providing all manner of store. . . .
> Happy the people to whom such blessings fall!
> Happy the people whose God is the LORD!"
>                    —Psalm 144:13, 15

The New Testament takes the Isaiah invitation one step farther. Physical nourishment is used as a metaphor for a different kind of food. We see this in the Sermon on the Mount, "Is not life more than food?" (Matt. 6:25), and in Jesus' answer when his disciples implored him to eat, "I have food to eat of which you do not know. . . . My food is to do the will of him who sent me, and to accomplish his work" (John 4:32, 34).

This is not to imply that the New Testament is totally unconcerned about the uses of food. Mealtimes figure prominently in the life of Jesus, often providing the occasion for important teaching. Jesus was concerned about seeing that his followers were fed, even when it meant breaking the laws of the Pharisees (Matt. 12:1–8) or suspending the laws of nature (Matt. 14:13–21) or preparing breakfast with his own hands in one of his resurrection appearances (John 21:9–14). In fact, nearly all of Jesus' resurrection appearances are connected with eating. It was in the familiar, homely act of "the breaking of the bread" (Luke 24:35) that the disciples recognized him at Emmaus, and it was by eating broiled fish (Luke 24:43) that he provided proof to his followers of the corporeal reality of the resurrection.

Jesus does not speak of how to use food wisely. He does not mention "comfort food" or nutrition. Of course, he may have encouraged the disciples to eat those whole-grain ears of wheat in order to get their fiber requirements, but there is no biblical record of such a concern. Jesus used food to meet physical needs, to show compassion toward others, to celebrate with friends (even at the risk of being accused of gluttony), and as a metaphor in his teaching. Some of his most powerful images of the kingdom of God are couched in terms of banquets and feasts: the marriage feast (Luke 14:7–14), the great banquet (Luke 14:15–24), the lost son (Luke 15:11–32).

Jesus even spoke of himself as food: "I am the bread of life; whoever comes to me shall not hunger, and whoever believes in me shall never thirst" (John 6:35, RSV alt.); "This is my body which is given for you" (Luke 22:19).

Jesus' primary concern seemed that the matter of eating be kept in proper perspective. His words, "Do not be anxious about your life, what you shall eat . . . your Father knows that you need [these things]" (Luke 12:22, 30), remind us again that God is the giver of good gifts. Too much anxiety indicates that we do not truly believe this and therefore live lives that are characterized by worry rather than thanksgiving.

In Paul's writings we find a different perspective on food. Although he did not speak of calories and cholesterol, he was concerned about dietary laws and spoke in several passages about the appropriate use of food.

In the eighth chapter of 1 Corinthians, Paul is trying to help the Corinthian Christians understand that it is all right for them to eat meat that has been offered to idols. There were two ways in which this might happen, apart from taking part in pagan rituals. Meat not consumed in the sacrifices was frequently taken home by the worshipers and eaten there, and a Christian might be invited to dine with a family where this meat was served. It was also a common practice for such meat to be sold in the markets. Paul argues that because the gods to which the meat has been offered do not really exist, meat offered to them is in no way supernaturally "tainted" but is neutral. "We are no worse off if we do not eat, and no better off if we do" (v. 8). But he hastens to add that although we are free to eat, we are also free *not* to eat, when doing so might adversely affect someone else. Calvin said, "this liberty is made subject to love" and further adds that sobriety and moderation are well-pleasing to God.[5] Therefore, self-denying love becomes the rule of thumb for Christians who are trying to decide how to eat appropriately.

The same theme is found in Romans, when Paul uses "walking in love" as a way to describe how to determine the limits of our freedom. He warns that we must not get so caught up in reveling in this "freedom to eat anything" that we forget what is of primary importance: that "the kingdom of God does not mean food and drink but righteousness and peace and joy in the Holy Spirit" (Rom. 14:17).

In 1 Corinthians 10, Paul reminds us that food is God's gift. He quotes a familiar verse from the psalms: "The earth is the Lord's and everything in it" (v. 26). Then once again he elaborates the theme of inward freedom when it comes to eating, but adds a criterion that lies outside ourselves: the glory of God (v. 31). Is this simply a cliché? On the lips of many it would be, but for Paul it was a matter of devotion and service to those in the Christian community and to those still outside it. Eating to the glory of God has a far deeper implication than dieting for the sake of good health. It implies that eating is also one of the ways in which we show our concern and love for others, and a way in which we can witness to the reality of our faith. As Calvin puts it so well:

> He teaches that there is no part of life and no action so minute that it ought not to be directed to the glory of God, and that we must take care that, even in eating and drinking, we may aim at the advancement of it. . . . It was well expressed in a common proverb, that we must not live to eat, but eat to live. Provided the end of living be at the same time kept in view, the consequence will thus be, that our food will be in a manner sacred to God, inasmuch as it will be set apart for his service.[6]

The ultimate rationale for the sacramental understanding of life expressed by Calvin is found in the second letter to the Corinthians, where Paul reminds us that "we are the temple of the living God" (2 Cor. 6:16). The word used is not the general word for temple, *hieron*, but the word reserved for the inner sanctuary, the *naos*, the Holy of Holies, where God's presence was most especially felt. That's us, with our feet of clay and our readiness to eat forbidden fruit. Eating to the glory of God means letting God's presence be tangibly revealed in our most ordinary acts. "Let us then pursue what makes for peace and for mutual upbuilding. Do not, for the sake of food, destroy the work of God" (Rom. 14:19–20).

The New Testament understanding of food builds on what has been expressed in the rich tradition of the Old Testament: that food is the gift of a loving God who provides for our needs and that, because of this, gratitude and not anxiety should be our response. It adds a new dimension to the Old Testament dietary laws: that we are free to eat anything so long as we walk in love, that our eating habits are a reflection of our relationship to God, and that food serves as a meaningful metaphor for basic insights into the kingdom of God. Isaiah spoke of the food that will make your soul live (55:2–3), but Jesus spoke of the "bread which comes down from heaven, that a man may eat . . . and not die" (John 6:50) and identified that bread with himself.

The final summary is given beautifully by James: "Every good gift and every perfect present comes from heaven; it comes down from God, the Creator of the heavenly lights, who does not change or cause darkness by turning" (James 1:17, TEV).

### FOOD FOR THOUGHT

André Simon, president of the Wine and Food Society, wrote:

> "For close upon two thousand years Christians of all denominations have had and still have one prayer in common—the Lord's Prayer; they all ask, as they were divinely ordered to do, that they may be given their daily bread, even before asking to be forgiven their trespasses, to be delivered from evil, and not to be led into temptation."[7]

What is your response to God's good gift of food? Is it just something whose "dailyness" you take for granted, or is your gratitude demonstrated in the way you use it?

RECIPES FOR ACTION

1.  How do you express gratitude to God for food? Is table grace routine and perfunctory, or does it truly express your sense of being "strangely sustained, nurtured, and nourished," as Brueggemann expresses it? Take time to think about your pattern of giving thanks and talk it over with the family. Has the beauty and power of table grace been lost by reducing it to a game of "Whose turn is it?" or a chance to show off the children's ability to recite "God is great"? Are there ways family members could participate more thoughtfully, perhaps by naming foods for which each is particularly thankful?

  Spend a few minutes writing out several table graces that reflect your feeling about God's good gift.

2.  How do our eating habits reflect our relationship to God? Take a piece of paper and jot down any eating habits of yours that indicate a careless stewardship of God's good gifts. Now list at least three things you or your family could do to treat food more "sacramentally."

3.  "Bread is made for laughter," the book of Ecclesiastes says. Plan a specific way to have fun with food this week: a picnic, making special cookies, or preparing someone's favorite menu and delivering it. Spice your food with a smile!

4.  Close your eyes and think about the petition in the Lord's Prayer: "Give us this day our daily bread." Draw the images that come to your mind.

  Now think of African children dying of hunger. Or a homeless person in a soup kitchen. Or a single mother with five children. What would this prayer mean to them? What is the difference in the prayer for you and for these others?

5.  What does the metaphor of "God the Gardener" mean to you? Write down three specific gifts God has given you. What has been your response?

# 3    HOSPITALITY

## *Expression of Grace*

The guest while in the house is its Lord.
  —Ancient Arabic proverb

Hospitality. The word conjures up various images for us: white tablecloths, candles, and RSVP invitations. A backyard barbecue. Christmas open house. A cup of coffee with a neighbor. The whole idea has fallen on hard times. Busy schedules, working mothers, the disappearance of servants, and the rise of a highly mobile population have combined to make genuine hospitality seem a thing of the past. We wistfully think of the "good old days," when neighbors dropped by or when company for supper was a regular occurrence. Was hospitality just a passing fad, now obsolete, its usefulness over? The Bible doesn't think so.

The Old Testament places much emphasis on hospitality. It was not an option in the life of Semitic peoples but a moral obligation. We find Job boasting about never failing to give hospitality to the wayfarer (31:32). The harshness of desert life made nomadic people sensitive to the needs of those who appeared at their tents seeking food and shelter.

Hospitality was seen as a holy duty, an expression of righteousness, not only among the people of God but among followers of other religions as well. An ancient Babylonian poem reads:

Give food to eat,
give wine to drink . . . ;
with him who thus acts
his god is pleased,
he is pleasing to Shamash,
he will requite him with good.''[1]

In New Testament times, hospitality had a different flavor. Inns and hostels on the network of Roman roads offered places to stay, which lessened the importance of private accommodations. The strong sense of community loyalty was breaking down and, with it, the practice of hospitality. Although the Romans gave lavish banquets, it was not their custom to offer hospitality to wandering strangers. They were more influenced by the Stoic ideal of self-sufficiency than the Old Testament understanding of hospitality as a moral obligation.

By the second century, hospitality had become something of a burden. The result was that people had to be reminded to show hospitality, as in Hebrews 13:2—''Do not neglect to show hospitality to strangers, for thereby some have entertained angels unawares''—which is quite recognizably a reference to the well-known story of Abraham's hospitality. First Peter 4:9 echoes this: ''Practice hospitality ungrudgingly to one another.'' Being hospitable was included in the list of attributes especially important for bishops (1 Tim. 3:2) and for widows (1 Tim. 5:10).

Jewish travelers seeking hospitality could find it at the synagogue. After the service, it was the custom for the worshipers to invite visitors home with them for a meal. Examples of this are in the story of Paul and Lydia (Acts 16:13–15) and in the account of Jesus being received as a guest by the Pharisee (Luke 14:1). As this practice became more and more common, hospitality became more predictable. Almost certainly there would be a stranger at worship to whom one could extend an invitation.

As hospitality became less impromptu, it began to acquire rules. Invitations became more formal, not only for Sabbath entertaining but for other times as well.

Banquets, weddings, social occasions: all acquired an etiquette. The parable of the great banquet (Luke 14:15–24)) describes one such formal occasion of hospitality.

There were, however, times of open hospitality when everyone was invited. It was the custom to signal these "open to everyone" occasions by hanging a cloth or pennant on the door or by simply leaving the door ajar. Sometimes a servant was sent out into the streets to bring in the crowds (see Luke 14:23). Etiquette required the guest to refuse the invitation at first and the host to insist that the guest accept. The disciples on the Emmaus road "constrained" or "compelled" Jesus to eat with them. This does not mean they used force but, rather, that they insisted on his spending the evening in accordance with this custom.

The understanding of hospitality as a result of the gracious activity of God was carried over into the life of the early church, where it was identified as a gift of the Spirit. The church was expected to provide for the needs of the traveling missionaries and preachers. The list of exhortations in Romans 12 includes "Contribute to the needs of the saints, practice hospitality" (v. 13).

THE GUEST MEAL

In Semitic culture the primary idea associated with hospitality has always been the bestowal of food. The central element of hospitality in Old Testament times, therefore, was the "guest meal." The classic example of the guest meal is the story of Abraham and Sarah entertaining the three angels with calf, curds, and milk (Gen. 18:1–16). Another guest meal is described in Judges 19:20–21 when the old Gibeonite invited the visiting Ephraimite Levite stranger to his home with these words: "Peace be to you; I will care for all your wants; only, do not spend the night in the square." The passage goes on, "So he brought him into his house, and gave the asses provender; and they washed their feet, and ate and drank." Other stories of guest meals are: Lot entertaining two angels and providing a feast, unleavened bread, and shelter (Gen. 19:1–11); Elijah being served water and bread by the widow of Zarephath (1 Kings 17:8–16); and the Shunammite woman providing Elisha with food and shelter (2 Kings 4:8–10). The guest meal was primarily hospitality extended to strangers, not to friends.

J. B. Mathews, in his unpublished dissertation, describes the patterned ritual of the guest meal.[2]

> *The Greeting.* This was highly formalized. It began with a word of blessing, "Shalom." The stranger was addressed as "my lord," and the host described himself as the guest's servant (see the Abraham and Lot stories just mentioned).
>
> *The Gesture.* The host offered a kiss, or an embrace, or a handclasp as a gesture of obeisance.
>
> *Washing.* Water for washing hands or feet was provided (see Judges 19:21).
>
> *Seating.* The guest was seated in the place of honor next to the host. If the host wished to give special honor to the guest, the host stood until invited to sit by the guest.
>
> *The Meal.* Prepared by women, who usually did not join the men at the table, the meal was usually roast beef or lamb (not a part of the ordinary daily diet), bread or cakes, wine and milk. An example is the meal prepared for Saul by the woman of Endor (1 Sam. 28:24).
>
> *The Farewell.* Often there was a farewell feast, during which a final libation was drunk, blessings were exchanged, and gifts presented to the guest. Many times the guest was sent off with an escort, sometimes the host himself.
>
> *Host's Duty.* The host was to provide for all the guest's needs and the needs of the guest's animals, to guard the guest's life for three days (the length of time the first meal was thought to stay in the stomach), and to make gifts to the guest at departure time.
>
> *Guest's Duty.* Protocol required the guest to arrive before sunset; to express satisfaction with the food, but not to eat it all; and to offer no payment, for that was considered an insult.

The guest-meal ritual was still practiced in New Testament times, although no specific description has been handed down in early writings. Many elements are the same as in Old Testament practices: the greeting, seating the guest in the place of honor, hand and foot washing, leaving a portion of food to express satisfaction.

It was customary for the head of the household to speak the words of blessing, break the bread and distribute it, then take a piece and eat it. The guests would follow his example. The blessing used by the host was probably the familiar Jewish prayer: "Blessed art thou, O Lord our God, king of the world, who bringest forth bread from the earth."

The common grace ended the meal, usually with these words: "Blessed be the God of the universe whose bounty we have eaten." It was customary for the guest to be asked to give this prayer, and to add to it a prayer for the host: "May it be God's will that our host may never be ashamed in this world nor disgraced in the next world." If wine was served at this point, the required blessing of the wine would be combined with this common grace.

As the guest departed, etiquette required the guest to express thanks and the host to bless the guest with the words "Go in peace."

## GOD AS HOST

Old Testament hospitality was marked by another element that lifted it above the realm of simple human kindness and generosity. The guest meal was not only festal but had a sacrificial nature as well. Killing an animal was regarded as a sacrificial act. Therefore, when meat was eaten on festal occasions, such as the guest meal, it carried sacred significance. Even the bread cakes, the second most important ingredient of the guest meal, were associated with sacrificial feasts (see 2 Sam. 6:19). In sacrificial meals, the people and their God came together at the same table to partake of the same holy food. Eating together resulted in being drawn together, in a renewal of the covenant bond.

Hospitality, therefore, became an expression of the covenant relationship with God and with other human beings. The embrace, the gifts, the protection of the life of the guest—all are concrete manifestations of living together in harmony. The guest is accepted into the family community and receives food, not only for the body but for the soul. Through fellowship, story sharing, and being welcomed, the guest goes forth renewed and restored.

Through our hospitality, it is possible to imitate God's loving care. Our compassion and pity mirror God's grace. Another Arabic proverb says, "The one who has bread is debtor to the one who has none." When we have received God's blessing of food, we bestow that blessing on others by sharing it with them; we *owe* it to them.

The image of God as host was used often by Jesus in his parables, notably the marriage feast (Matt. 22:1–14), the great banquet (Luke 14:15–24), and the lost son (Luke 15:11–32). In these parables Jesus, too, calls us to be a host in the way in which God is host. The parables and other New Testament passages define for us what that means.

> To be a host as God is host is to disrupt hierarchical protocol by inviting those who cannot repay you. "When you give a feast, invite the poor" (Luke 14:13).
>
> To be a host as God is host is to kill the fatted calf for the guest who least deserves it (Luke 15:32).
>
> To be a host as God is host means providing hospitality that is without restraint, unbounded, not measured, generous, without payment, cheerful, and valid at all times and in all circumstances. "Welcome one another . . . as Christ has welcomed you" (Rom. 15:7).
>
> To be a host means to be a part of the mutual blessing that comes from table fellowship. "Show hospitality to strangers, for thereby some have entertained angels unawares" (Heb. 13:2).
>
> To be a host is contributing to shalom, the wholeness and peace which

characterize community at its deepest level. "Today salvation has come to this house" (Luke 19:9).

## HOSPITALITY
## TO THE STRANGER

Both the Old and New Testaments stress that the primary recipient of hospitality is to be the "stranger." However, strangers are not necessarily those different in culture, race, or socioeconomic status. They may be members of our family, or friends or neighbors who have become alienated from us.[3]

When we offer hospitality to strangers, some curious and unexpected results occur. Thomas Ogletree and Parker Palmer have both written on the implications of this form of hospitality. In *Hospitality to a Stranger*, Ogletree says:

> To offer hospitality to a stranger is to welcome something new, unfamiliar, and unknown into our life-world. Strangers have stories to tell which we have never heard before, stories which can redirect our seeing and stimulate our imaginations.[4]

Parker Palmer has a similar thought when he writes, "Hospitality to the stranger gives us a chance to see our own lives afresh."[5] Genuine hospitality to the stranger calls us to do the following:

Value the strangeness of the stranger, accepting the differences between us without fear, annoyance, or distrust. The guest is not someone for whom we are doing a favor, but one who is honoring us.

See ourselves through the eyes of the stranger and either be affirmed or be willing to learn and change because of what has been revealed to us about ourselves. The Christmas International House program sponsored by the Presbyterian Church (U.S.A.), which brings international students into American homes for the Christmas holidays, frequently has this result in people's lives.

Recognize that we are strangers too. God's faithful people have always been "strangers and exiles on the earth" (Heb. 11:13). The classic model of hospitality, Abraham, was himself a "wandering Aramean," a "stranger in a strange land," when he welcomed the three visitors who came to his door.

Bring about reconciliation and renewal for the one who is alien or lost.

And, finally, even extend hospitality to God by showing lovingkindness to those in need. Jesus makes this plain in Matthew 25 with his words, "As you did it to one of the least of these my brethren, you did it to me (v. 40).

## FOOD FOR THOUGHT

John Scott has written a moving prayer-poem that describes what can happen when we learn to reach out to strangers with the gift of hospitality:

We respond to your invitation, O God. As we are, we come. We offer to you the hostilities that shape us, the hostilities we carry, the hostilities that carry us. In these matters, move us from hostility to hospitality.

Be our guard, for we guard ourselves too much. Be our protector, that we need not overprotect ourselves.

Create in us a space, a room, a place—a free and friendly space where the stranger may be welcomed

—that we may be at home in our own house.

—that we may be healed of the hurts we carry in the soul.

—that we may know brother and sisterhood.

—that we may know kindness.

—that we may laugh easily.

—that we may know beauty.

—Nudge, guide, entice, prod. Move us to live within your will. To the end that within this flesh, within this house in which we live, we may be at home with you, with our neighbor, with ourselves.

Thus we pray, remembering Christ who says, "I stand at the door and knock." Create in us a place of hospitality.
Amen.[6]

Where does the biblical understanding of hospitality as a moral obligation fit into our busy lives? How can we learn to honor the other, receive the stranger's gift of new sight, bring about reconciliation, and be a host to God? It would be far easier to retreat into the seductive environment described by Ray Bradbury in his 1953 novel, *Fahrenheit 451*. In this story, people have fled from one another into living rooms whose walls are TV screens. When they are together, they avoid conversation by plugging their ears with transistor radios. The narrator hero begins to realize that this lifestyle is making him a "silly empty man" living with a "silly empty woman."

This painful picture written almost four decades ago is no longer science fiction. People jog past one another, or sit in doctors' waiting rooms side by side, ears plugged with what Bradbury prophetically described as "electronic bees humming the hour away." No exchange of greetings, no acknowledgment that another human being is anywhere near. No time for pausing to hear the stranger's story. We distrust strangers; we do not want to make ourselves open or vulnerable to those we do not know. There is the fear of being taken advantage of. We live in a hostile society, and yet, as Lynne Hundley writes, "when I am willing to risk the eating, the walking, the sharing, there will be no more strangers."[7]

Although biblical hospitality is primarily concerned with strangers, we must not forget that strangers are sometimes those most closely related to us. God had to remind the covenant people, "Do not refuse to help your own relatives" (Isa. 58:7, TEV). Henri Nouwen speaks of the need for parents to offer their own children hospitality. Although it sounds strange, Nouwen defines this kind of hospitality as providing a place of acceptance, support, and encouragement where children can ask questions without fear of rejection.[8]

Where do we begin in our effort to reclaim biblical hospitality in our lives? In recent years, several excellent books have offered concrete and helpful suggestions for individuals, families, and churches. Doris Janzen Longacre has written *Living More with Less*, a compilation of suggestions from Mennonites around the world about achieving a more Christian lifestyle. Marlene Lefever's *Creative Hospitality* (Wheaton, Ill.: Tyndale House, 1986) is a book of ideas for ways to extend Christian hospitality to both friends and strangers. These ideas include a housewarming, a Passover celebration, a "recycled Christmas party," a neighborhood drop-in, and dozens of others. Many are related directly to developing a sense of community in the church family; others are ways to extend hospitality to strangers.

RECIPES FOR ACTION

1.  Does the ritual of the guest meal suggest changes you might make in the way you think of hospitality? Is a guest "lord" while in your home? Is hospitality a growth experience for you? A primary form of entertainment and pleasure in your life? A moral obligation? Write down one thing hospitality means to you.

2.  Think of simple ways to show hospitality. Start with the people next door. How long has it been since you invited them over for an evening of soup and bread and sharing slides? Or a game of croquet on the lawn with lemonade and oatmeal cookies? List three specific ways you could show hospitality to people with whom you brush shoulders every day.

3.  Extend your horizons. We all have "gate places" in our lives where we encounter strangers who need our hospitality: at school, work, in the neighborhood, at PTA, at church. Go to these places or gatherings as the covenant people of God did, armed with the expectation that you will invite home a stranger. Look forward to hearing the stranger's story. Be ready for a challenge to your old ways of thinking. Be ready to receive as well as give.

4.  "Open your homes to the homeless poor" (Isa. 58:7, TEV). List the agencies and churches that provide food for the homeless. How can you help? The homeless include those who are temporarily displaced. Are there international students or refugees in your community who would welcome an invitation to your home for a typical American meal?

5.  Don't forget the family. What are three things you might do to treat your children, or other family members, as guests? Review once again the ritual for the guest meal. One suggestion: Listen to their stories.

# 4            BONDING

## *Strangers No Longer*

Spread the table and the quarrel will end.
>—Hebrew proverb

At a banquet Wisdom may renew its moral forces. The bonds of society become narrowed, and rivals or enemies are merged into friends or guests. Persons who are entire strangers to each other share in the intimacy of the family, differences in rank are wiped out, weakness is united to power, manners are polished, and the mind takes fresh flight.
>—A. Beauvilliers, *L'art du cuisinier* (1814)

They had their meals together in their homes, eating with glad and humble hearts, praising God, and enjoying the good will of all the people.
>—Acts 2:46–47, TEV

Near Americus, Georgia, there is a community known as Koinonia Partners, founded five decades ago by Clarence Jordan. The members of this group have dedicated themselves to "compassionate living," an intentional effort to live out the teachings of Christ in communal love and service. One of the marks of this community is the coming together for a simple noonday meal. An old-fashioned farm bell rings, and everyone gathers in a large dining room whose walls are adorned with peace posters, Christian banners, and notices about community events. There are babies in high chairs, elderly folk in work boots and straw hats, young volunteers from all over the world. When the meal is finished, there is a meditation time led by a member of the community and a time for the sharing of concerns and prayer. This mealtime experience is of central importance to the life of the community. The bonding that occurs as the community eats, worships, and shares its concerns is a vital part of the glue that holds the community together.

Most of us have experienced this kind of bonding in some form: at family reunions when distant cousins discover one another, at church suppers where new members are welcomed into the church family, at a picnic for the newcomers on the block, at a quiet dinner with old friends. In the breaking of bread together, something happens. Ordinary meals become sacramental occasions. Strangers become companions, a word whose literal meaning is "the one with whom bread is broken."

This is profoundly biblical. Relationships in the Old Testament were affirmed by breaking bread together. Pacts were sealed with meals. The covenant was reaffirmed by ritual feast times. The Hebrew word for "covenant" (*berith*) possibly had its origin in the Hebrew word meaning "to eat."

In the New Testament, too, there are numerous occasions when eating together was used as a symbol of unity. The sharing of food is a central theme in the New Testament, especially in Luke's writings (it is mentioned 31 times in Luke, 26 in Mark, 20 in Matthew, and 14 in John). In 1 Corinthians, eating is a central theological issue and is mentioned by Paul 22 times. The primary example of the bonding power of food is seen in the celebration of the Lord's Supper, a meal that became a symbol of unity in the faith, not only to the early Christians but for all Christians down through the ages.

By looking at the biblical understanding of the relationship between eating and bonding, perhaps we can regain a respect for the way in which sharing food becomes a bridge between strangers, reduces hostility, strengthens family ties, and brings a glimpse of shalom into a fragmented and disjointed world.

PERSONAL OR TRIBAL BONDING

There are many instances in the Old Testament where pacts or treaties were sealed by the parties sharing a common meal. Consuming food together made the participants symbolically members of the same family or clan. Some examples of these pacts are:

Abraham and Melchizedek, the priest-king of Salem, celebrating their alliance with bread and wine (Gen. 14:18–20)

Isaac confirming his peace treaty with Abimelech by preparing a feast during which "they ate and drank" and swore an oath to keep the agreement (Gen. 26:30)

Jacob and Laban settling their long-standing differences with a covenant of peace and sealing the pact with an all-night picnic on a mountain (Gen. 31:54)

The Gibeonites, fearing Joshua after he had conquered Jericho and Ai, resorting to trickery to avoid a confrontation (by pretending they were strangers from far away, they persuaded Joshua and his men to eat a covenant meal with them; as a result of the bond established by eating together, Joshua could not kill them even when the trickery was revealed; Josh. 9:3–15)

Aaron and all the elders of Israel eating bread with Jethro, Moses' father-in-law, after fleeing from Egypt (it is possible that this meal symbolized the admission of the Israelites into blood kinship with the Midianites; Ex. 18:12)

THE COVENANT OF SALT

It was not necessary to eat a full meal for the bonding to occur. It could also be done by simply eating salt together. Eating salt with another was a way to indicate a bond of loyalty. God's promise to Aaron in Numbers 18:19 was described as a "covenant of salt," meaning an unbreakable or permanent covenant.

Even when Jesus spoke the words "Have salt in yourselves," he may have been referring to the covenant of salt, reminding his disciples of the importance of their loyalty and devotion to one another. This is particularly significant in light of the last part of the sentence, which says, "and be at peace with one another" (Mark 9:50). The admonition in Colossians 4:6 ("Let your speech always be . . . seasoned with salt") may also refer to the symbolic power of salt to create unity and harmony.

This custom has persisted into modern times. The story is told of a Scot who was captured by an Arab sheikh and who, like the Gibeonites, used trickery to get the sheikh to eat salt with him. By doing so, he became the Arab's guest, bound by one of the strongest ties of desert hospitality, the covenant of salt, and so was safe from harm.

### CULTIC BONDING

The cultic sacrifices of the Old Testament represented another type of bonding by food. The primary and original purpose of sacrifice among the Semitic people seems to have been to cement relations with a god by sharing a meal with that god. It is certainly evident that the Israelites thought of themselves as being in a covenant relationship with God and felt that God participated in their communal feasts. In the story of Jethro's feast, there were sacrifices to God, but bread was also eaten "before God," as if God were the host at the meal. Similarly, after the Israelites went into Canaan, they were commanded to make sacrifices and "eat before the LORD your God" (Deut. 12:7).

Roland de Vaux describes a particular type of sacrifice in ancient Israel, which, through thanksgiving to God, brings about union with God. He calls this type of sacrifice "communion sacrifice" and says its characteristic feature lies in the fact that the victim is shared by God, the priest, and the person offering the sacrifice. Eating the sacrifice is a holy act, which may be shared by the person's family or by invited guests, but only if they too are in a state of ritual purity. The idea of communion with God as an integral part of the covenant was thus given tangibility in the symbolic act.[1]

It is possible that this understanding of union with God was behind the Passover stipulation that each member of the household must eat at least an olive-sized portion of the Paschal lamb, which had been consecrated or offered to God. In this way they renewed their bond with the One who shared the meal.

## EATING WITH OUTCASTS

One of the radical elements of Jesus' ministry was his willing association with those outside the pale of Jewish legalism. He received much criticism for this from the scribes and Pharisees, and this criticism was especially sharp when they saw him eating with those who did not observe the Jewish law. Sharing a meal with nonobservers of the Torah was condemned by the rabbis.

At the time of Christ, there was a class of people whom the doctors of the Law detested and against whom they preached scorn and hatred. They were called the *'am ha'aretz*, the "people of the land." They were, in part, descendants of the Canaanites, or of the invading forces who had occupied the Holy Land for so many years: Assyrians, Arameans, Philistines, etc. Although circumcised, they did not practice the law. The formal definition of the *'am ha'aretz*, in the Talmud is: "He who does not eat his bread in a state of ritual cleanliness." Galilee was a center for the *'am ha'aretz*, and it is no wonder that they responded eagerly to the teachings of Christianity with its message of grace and its deemphasis on the Law. It gave them an opportunity to be included, to "sit at table," to be a part of the family.

Christ's message came as a turning upside-down of accepted religious practices. Those who were considered unclean were to be invited to share in table fellowship and thereby to be accepted as kin. Hospitality was not to be based on reciprocity, or extended only to those in certain life strata, but was to be continuous, inclusive, and generous. This message was a radical new interpretation of kinship bonding in the kingdom of God.

One example of this inclusive hospitality is seen in the story of Levi's feast in Luke 5. Levi was a publican, a tax collector or customs house official in the service of the Romans. As such, he represented a group of people much despised by the religious hierarchy. Not only was he a collaborator with the occupation forces but he was a "sinner" as well, meaning one who did not keep all the ceremonial observances laid down by rabbis. In commenting on this passage, biblical scholar William Arndt says that to be someone's companion at the table was looked upon as "constituting a high degree of intimacy" and makes the point that while this was not expressly forbidden in the Torah, it was a part of the tradition developed by the rabbis to protect the Law. This tradition, or midrash, had come to possess the same validity in the minds of the scribes and Pharisees as the Law itself.[2] To see a rabbi reclining at the table of a publican and sinner horrified these "righteous" onlookers, and they immediately began to attack him. Jesus' answer clearly sets forth his understanding of the inclusive nature of his ministry.

By sharing a meal with a publican who did not observe the law, Jesus was giving a parabolic answer to the question, "Who is my mother and who are my brothers?" Levi had responded to the call of Christ, and that faithful response made him a part of his family.

A similar bond is made with another publican, Zacchaeus, when Jesus goes to his home. Although no mention is made of a feast, it is clear that staying in Zacchaeus' house would involve eating a meal together. Once more, Jesus' love reached out in a dramatic way to one who was despised and shunned by the leaders of the religious community.

BONDING
AT THE LORD'S TABLE

The primary example of the bonding power of the shared meal is, as we have said, the Lord's Supper. The occasion was the Passover, a sacred meal whose purpose was to weld families together in their allegiance to the one true God who had delivered them. Why, then, did Jesus not celebrate the Passover with his own family? Why did he observe this special feast with the twelve disciples instead? Could it have been Jesus' intent to cement the bonds between himself and his friends in preparation for the difficult days ahead? Joseph Grassi thinks so and suggests that Jesus' choosing to celebrate this supper with his disciples "constituted a new solidarity that transcended family bonds and sometimes even opposed them. Jesus' sharing of bread and wine was an effective symbol that *every* man and woman could be brother and sister and thus share together the earth's resources."[3]

Judas' betrayal is all the more poignant because of the betrayal by one whose hand was with Jesus' "on the table." There is an echo of the grief expressed in Psalm 41:9: "Even my bosom friend in whom I trusted, who ate of my bread, has lifted his heel against me." The sacred bond of the table, the commitment to loyalty and kinship, was being broken, and Jesus, looking deep into the heart of Judas, knew it.

John tells us that after Judas had left, Jesus began to speak to the disciples, and a recurrent theme in his words is that of the special bond they shared.

> By this all men will know that you are my disciples, if you have love for one another. . . . If you love me, you will keep my commandments. . . . In that day you will know that I am in my Father, and you in me, and I in you. . . . Abide in me and I in you. . . . No longer do I call you servants . . . but I have called you friends. . . . All mine are thine, and thine are mine, and I am glorified in them. . . . I in them and thou in me, that they may become perfectly one.
> —John 13:35; 14:15, 20; 15:4, 15; 17:10, 23

Paul understood clearly the significance of the Lord's Supper as a symbol of unity and kinship. In the tenth chapter of 1 Corinthians, a very food-oriented chapter, Paul speaks of the cup of blessing and the breaking of bread as being a partnership (koinonia) of the body of Christ, a phrase that has resulted in much theological debate. The blessing in Jewish worship means that the cup has been offered to God. This blessing, then, makes the cup the Lord's cup and the partakers drink as guests of the Lord. Therefore, eating the bread and drinking the wine as Christ's guests bonds the partakers with Christ and with each other.

"Because there is one bread, we who are many are one body, for we all partake of the one bread" (1 Cor. 10:17). Eating together bonds together.

The medieval scholar John Colet wrote some beautiful and expressive words about this verse: "In the blessed cup and the broken bread is a saving communication of the true body and blood itself of Jesus Christ, shared by many that in it they may be one. These many are united in the sharing of the One, and in the being formed anew into it."[4]

The reference to the Old Testament ritual in verse 18 uses another curious phrase: "partners in the altar." It seems to mean that when the people made sacrifices as gifts to God, God was pleased and, in turn, gave them portions of the sacrifice so they might share in the feast at the altar. The Greek word used for a meal, *deipnon,* had a cultic meaning as well as a secular one; it signified the union of those who eat with the deity. Thus as table fellowship was established with God, the participants were established as God's people. In a similar manner, says Paul, we establish our oneness with Jesus as we eat the eucharistic meal. In assimilating the food, we acquire a new identity.

Wendy Wright makes a beautiful connection between the communion meal and a mother nursing her child:

> I have often thought that the communion meal that our Christian faith celebrates is best understood through reference to this art of giving learned in the nursing bond. As a people of faith we share bread and wine with one another. We enter into a ritual that bespeaks our true life as a community of mutual need and nourishment. . . . We are called to be food and drink for one another, to give life, to share the substance of who we are, to have our deepest resources tapped so that the whole community can begin to realize something of the fullness of life that Jesus holds out as hope and *is.*[5]

The strange thing about the Lord's table, unlike the Passover feast, is that the outcasts are there. Markus Barth makes a point of this in his book *Rediscovering the Lord's Supper.* We may not choose our companions at the Lord's table; they may be "bums," as Barth says, but we become bonded to them when we sit at table together. Barth reminds us that when we begin deciding that others are "too bad, too base, too little, too far removed from salvation" to be fit dinner companions at Jesus' table, then we do not "see, accept, and believe Jesus as he really is."[6]

## THE BONDED COMMUNITY

Luke continues his emphasis on food with a moving description of the early church community in Acts 2:42 and 46, which describes the community's sharing in fellowship meals and eating together with "glad and humble hearts" (TEV). The barriers between individuals had come down, and the community expressed its unity in the ancient way, by eating together. Their joy was probably accelerated by anticipation of the Lord's coming, but it no doubt had its root in the special bond they felt as they shared in prayer and fellowship together.

It is easy to romanticize the early church and forget the moments of divisiveness and disunity that plagued its beginnings. However, these two verses give us a nostalgic vision of a group of human beings who caught a glimpse of the kingdom of heaven as they broke bread together around a common table.

## FOOD FOR THOUGHT

One of the most memorable images in contemporary literature of the power of the common meal to bring unity into a community is found in Isak Dinesen's story "Babette's Feast," which has been made into an equally memorable movie. In this story, members of a grim and pious Scandanavian religious group become warm and loving toward one another through the transforming power of a great feast. A similar bonding takes place in Clyde Edgerton's novel *Walking Across Egypt,* when a friendship between a lonely woman and a troubled boy is initiated by her loving preparation of food for him.

Where did we go wrong? Why is it that in spite of modernized kitchens whose microwaves, food processors, freezers, salad shooters, and electric can openers make food preparation quick and efficient, mealtimes are sketchy, hasty, ill-planned, and disjointed? Family meals resemble relay races, making bonding all but impossible. People turn to places outside the home for a sense of belonging. We hear the longing for bondedness in the theme song of a popular television show: We all need a place to go "where everybody knows your name." If the family is no longer the matrix for bonding and common loyalty, then bonding must be found somewhere else.

One of these places can be the church. If we let the early church teach us about the importance of shared table fellowship, we will provide in our churches warm, solid gatherings that will extend hospitality to all and create bonds of unity, compassion, and understanding, renewing our commitment to one another. Ostensibly, that's the purpose of all church suppers, but something is lost when the preparation of the food overshadows the sharing that should take place around the table. Something is lost when strangers are never included in the conversation. Something is lost when only the older members of the congregation take the time to come. Something is lost when there is a boring "program" rather than time for genuinely getting acquainted. Something is lost when meals are catered, even when done to make it easier for working couples to come. Something is lost when we become apathetic about what it is that truly bonds us together and why it is important for us to celebrate the reality of the Christian community "at table." If we can recapture the spirit of the early church's agape meal, or love feast, we will have moved a long way toward healing the divisions in the church.

We also need to reclaim the Eucharist, and to recognize how this meal not only bonds Christians with other believers and with their Lord but calls us to the service of those who have no table: the world's poor. Cyprian wrote in the middle of the third century some words we need to hear again and again: "You are rich and wealthy and imagine that you celebrate the Lord's Supper without taking part in the offering. You come to the Lord's House with nothing to offer, suppressing the part of the sacrifice which belongs to the poor."[7]

RECIPES FOR ACTION

1. Help your minister plan a worship service that intentionally links the table of the Lord with the tables of the hungry, the poor, and the oppressed. Suggestions for resources may be found in *Bread for the World* by Arthur Simon, rev. ed. (New York: Paulist Press, 1985).

2. Who are the outcasts in your community? How can you share bread with them? Is there a shelter for the homeless or a soup kitchen for the hungry in your neighborhood? Can you not only serve them but break bread with them and hear their stories? Will you be willing to break down walls as Jesus did?

3. Offer to plan a church supper around the theme "Our Common Bonds." Post newsprint sheets around the room labeled with phrases such as the following or others appropriate for your group: "I was born in the South"; "I love the beach"; "My hobby is gardening"; "I love Italian food." List at least twelve categories, making them as comprehensive as possible so that everyone will find at least one category that fits. As people arrive, ask them to sign their names on all appropriate sheets. After supper, read aloud the names on each sheet, so that common bonds can be recognized. Ask the group to brainstorm other things that bond people together. Then ask, "What does it mean to be bonded together in Christ?" Put the answers on newsprint. Read Ephesians 4:1–6.

# 5     COMPASSION

## *The Great Inasmuch*

It is essential that both aspects of the broken bread be remembered: it is a symbol of spiritual nourishment, and it is a call for actual food for the hungry.

—Joseph Grassi

At a station in India

When I tried to eat,
suddenly
a small, dirty hand
came in front of me

and I saw the dark face
of a child
staring at me
with sunken eyes.

Embarrassed and even scared,
I put on his palm
a small piece of food and
quickly shut the window.

The train moved,
but his eyes kept

gazing at me—deeper
the more I pretended not seeing.

This of twenty years ago still
haunts me, and often
as I sit around the table
I feel his eyes gazing.
—Yorifumi Yaguchi


He who has a bountiful eye will be blessed,
for he shares his bread with the poor.
—Proverbs 22:9


God's good gifts are made to be shared. We extend hospitality to the stranger in the form of the guest meal, with its wine and meat and protection. We are bonded together in the process of sharing food. But there is more. In every age, in every place, as Jesus said, "The poor you have always with you." Their sunken eyes haunt us; their needs will not go away, even when our trains pull out of the station.[1]

This is not a new theme. It permeates the Bible. The Old Testament laws contained many provisions for the poor. Basic to these provisions was the understanding that compassion for the poor was not a call to charity but a simple demand for justice. In the New Testament, more of Jesus' words were devoted to issues of wealth and poverty, with numerous mentions of feeding the hungry, than to any other subject.

Somehow, though, we have blurred the importance of that intimate connection between our lip service to the gospel and the practice of compassion. Doris Janzen Longacre writes in *Living More with Less:*

Dare we even invite Christians from around the world to take a look at our church eating practices? Along with much good, they would also see:

Church cookbooks featuring fat- and sugar-rich salads and desserts: gooey variations of pink and green gelatin, cake and pudding mix, sour cream, nuts and whipped topping.

Overstuffed people standing in line at church supper tables groaning with pasta and fried foods.

Diet books in the church library.

A Food and Fellowship Committee doing a dinner with a missionary speaker, committee members losing sight of the meal's intent and nursing inflated notions of calamity—"What if we run out of rolls?" "What if the flowers don't arrive?"

Monday morning garbage by the church's back door: plastic bags gorged with Styrofoam cups and plates.

On the bulletin board: Christian Women's monthly luncheon at the Hilton East Room.[2]

A few years ago, after coming home from hunger-stricken Africa to affluent America, I expressed much the same feeling about what I saw:

I hear these words about "the poor"
and brush them into the corners of my mind.
I cannot think about them now
I am too preoccupied
   with the choice of hors d'oeuvres for my party
   and the color of my new shoes.
I am too anxious
   about the impression I make
   to decide for diminishing
   or to question the givens.
I am too cautious
   to risk the highway
   that leads away from safe places.
Convenience blankets me,
stifles the clamor of a hungry world.

In 1977, Ronald Sider wrote *Rich Christians in an Age of Hunger*, a watershed book about compassion. In it he quotes Robert Schuller's justification for the multimillion-dollar Garden Grove Community Church in California, which was superseded by the well-known Crystal Cathedral. Schuller responded to those who said he should have given the money to the poor by saying, "Suppose we had? What would we have today? We would still have hungry, poor people and God would not have this tremendous base of operations which He is using to inspire people to become more successful, more affluent, more generous, more genuinely unselfish in their giving of themselves."[3]

This is a rationalization many of us use to justify our affluent lifestyles. Sider then asks the hard questions: How much of our comfortable affluence is related to witnessing, and how much of it do we need to abandon in order to obey Jesus' commands to feed the poor? Are we really comfortable with Jesus' words: "It will be hard for a rich man to enter the kingdom of heaven" (Matt. 19:23)?

## COMPASSION AND JUSTICE IN THE OLD TESTAMENT

The Old Testament attitude toward hunger is a far cry from this kind of rationalization. Over and over again the theme of compassionate sharing is stressed.

In the manna story, this theme is clear. There were two miracles. The first is God's provision of the manna itself. When the children of Israel exclaimed in Hebrew, *"Man hu'?"* ("What is this?"), they were answered by Moses: "It is the bread which the LORD has given you to eat" (Ex. 16:15). The second occurred when the whole community was fed because people shared what they gathered. "Those who gathered much did not have too much, and those who gathered less did not have too little. Each had gathered just what he needed" (Ex 16:18, TEV).

To ensure that the rich did not keep on getting richer at the expense of the poor, the year of jubilee mandated that at the end of fifty years all land be returned to its original owners. It was as if God wanted to ensure the equality set up when the land was divided among the tribes. This incredible law underscored the principle that the land belonged to God and its users were merely stewards who cultivated it, enjoyed its harvest, and shared its resources (Lev. 25). This is not a question of philanthropy or generosity, but a mandate for justice. It was the right of the poor to receive back their land. Scholars are not clear as to whether the jubilee year was ever observed, since there are no references to it in the historical books, but Luke Johnson points out in his thoughtful work *Sharing Possessions* that Jesus based many of his difficult sayings about riches on this prophetic view of the use of the land.

In the same way, the prophets never appealed for charity or generosity from the rich but based their demand for justice on the principle that the earth and its resources belong to God and are merely lent to human beings, not for the benefit of a few but for all equally. Amos specifically denounced the fat "cows . . . who oppress the poor, who crush the needy, who say to their husbands, 'Bring, that we may drink!' "(4:1).

Justice was the core of the prophetic message. The prophets stressed the importance of knowing God and believed that to know God was to know a God of justice. Over and over again, they pointed out the connection between worship and justice. To a people who prided themselves on their scrupulous religious observances, the prophets' words must have sounded strange indeed:

> IsAIAH: "The kind of fasting I want is this: Remove the chains of oppression and the yoke of injustice, and let the oppressed go free. Share your food with the hungry" (58:6–7, TEV).
> AMOS: "I hate your religious festivals. . . . Instead, let justice flow like a stream, and righteousness like a river that never goes dry" (5:21, 24, TEV).
> JEREMIAH: "Stop believing those deceitful words, 'We are safe! This is the LORD's Temple, this is the LORD's Temple, this is the LORD's Temple!' Change the way you are living and stop doing the things you are doing. Be fair in your treatment of one another" (7:4–5, TEV).
> HOSEA: "I want your constant love, not your animal sacrifices" (6:6, TEV).

The law also provided for a sabbatical year. Every seven years the land was to lie fallow. The purpose of this was not only ecological but compassionate. In that year, the poor were free to gather for themselves whatever grew by itself. Once again, an institutionalized way was provided to lessen the gap between rich and poor. In commenting on this sabbatical year, Deuteronomy 15 makes the astonishing promise that no one will be poor if the law is carried out. Then the section ends with the realistic observation that because this is not likely to happen, there will always be those "who are poor and in need, so I command you to be generous to them" (15:11, TEV). It is this passage that Jesus was quoting when the disciples became angry over the waste of money by the woman with the alabaster jar of perfume. He wished to remind them of their responsibility to continue sharing with the poor.

Other Old Testament laws showed concern for feeding the hungry. The law on tithing required everyone to bring a tenth of their farm produce, which was then distributed to widows, orphans, Levites, and sojourners who had no land (Deut. 14:28–29). The laws for harvesters decreed that farmers should leave some of their harvest for the poor, including grapes that were accidentally dropped, and the corners of wheat fields (Lev. 19:9; 23:22; Deut. 24:19, 21). The story of Ruth is a familiar example of this gleaning.

The importance of sharing with the poor is a recurrent theme in Wisdom literature, too. Eliphaz is sure that Job must have "refused to feed those who were hungry" in order to merit his punishment. Job denies this charge, saying, "When the poor cried out, I helped them; I gave help to orphans who had nowhere to turn" (Job 22:7; 29:12, TEV).

The book of Proverbs contains many reminders of the importance of justice and compassion:

"Unused fields could yield plenty of food for the poor, but unjust men keep them from being farmed" (13:23, TEV).
"It is a disgrace to be greedy" (19:22, TEV).
"If you refuse to listen to the cry of the poor, your own cry for help will not be heard" (21:13, TEV).
"Be generous and share your food with the poor. You will be blessed for it" (22:9, TEV).

## COMPASSION AND JUSTICE
## IN THE NEW TESTAMENT

Compassion in the New Testament is perhaps best described by the almost unpronounceable Greek verb *splanchnizesthai*, which literally means "to have a churning of the insides." We find this word used of Jesus when he traveled in the towns and villages and saw the disease and sickness of those who came to him. When we read that the good Samaritan was "moved with pity" for the wounded man on the side of the road, the verb used is *esplanchnisthē* (Luke 10:34). This stomach-churning reaction comes not from a sense of duty but from compassion and identification with those in need. It breaks apart the word "compassion" into its components: "with passion." True compassion is deeply felt and results in action.

### Feeding of the Multitudes

Jesus' compassion was aroused again as he looked at the people gathered on that Galilean hillside who had followed him for three days. "My insides are churning for them," he said to his disciples (Matt. 15:32).

The familiar story of the loaves and fishes has several striking parallels to the manna story; the people were far from home in a desert place, without food, and seated in groups of fifties and hundreds that sound like the camps of the Israelites. Jesus' words, "You yourselves give them something to eat," echo the words of Moses to the children of Israel, "It is the bread which the LORD has given you to eat." Like the exodus story, the true miracle comes when the food is shared.

It is similar also to the Elisha story, which reinforces the idea that Jesus' words carry the weight of a prophetic command. Readers of the story in the early church would have regarded Jesus' words as a command to them. The Gospel of Matthew, which was designed to be a new Torah, is built around the central theme of Jesus' instructions and commands, especially to feed the hungry.

The multitudes are still waiting. As Jesus reminded us, the poor are always with us. Our five loaves and two fish seem paltry in the face of the world's hunger. And yet, the command has been given. The church has a responsibility to do what it can, motivated not by philanthropy and tax write-offs but by the simple, clear call for justice.

### The Inasmuch

Matthew 25 is a most uncomfortable chapter. It implies the unthinkable: that the sunken eyes of that child in India were the eyes of the Christ; that to ignore the swollen bellies of Africans, or the wretched men who line up at soup kitchens, is to ignore the one we claim to love with all our hearts. This passage actually dares to claim that service to the poor is service to God. It is the basis of the ministry of Mother Teresa, one of the ten most admired women in the world. She tells this story:

> A girl came from outside India to join the Missionaries of Charity. We have a rule that the very next day new arrivals must go to the Home for the Dying. So I told this girl: "You saw Father during Holy Mass, with what love and care he touched Jesus in the Host. Do the same when you go to the Home for the Dying, because it is the same Jesus you will find there in the broken bodies of our poor." And they went. After three hours the newcomer came back and said to me with a big smile—I have never seen a smile quite like that—"Mother, I have been touching the body of Christ for three hours." And I said to her: "How—what did you do?" She replied: "When we arrived there, they brought a man who had fallen into a drain, and been there for some time. He was covered with wounds and dirt and maggots, and I cleaned him and I knew I was touching the body of Christ."[4]

Ron Sider asks the question in an unforgettable way:

> What does it mean to feed and clothe the Creator of all things? We cannot know. We can only look on the poor and oppressed with new eyes and resolve to heal their hurts and help end their oppression. If Jesus' saying in Matthew 25:40 is awesome, its parallel is terrifying. "Truly, I say to you, as you did it not to one of the least of these, you did it not to me" (v. 45). What does that mean in a world where millions die each year while rich Christians live in affluence? What does it mean to see the Lord of the universe lying by the roadside starving and walk by

on the other side? We cannot know. We can only pledge, in fear and trembling, not to kill him again.[5]

It is impossible to miss the note of warning here. The passage is a description of the final judgment when what has been done for "the least important" will be what counts. It follows the parable of the talents that Arthur Simon of Bread for the World calls a parable about the arrogance of pretending to be powerless. We cannot use the excuse that the problem is too enormous and we are too weak. Instead, we root our hope in God and work for the kingdom, believing that our efforts are not in vain.

*The Common Purse*

In our fascination with Judas's dishonesty, we sometimes overlook the deeper significance of the money bag from which he helped himself. The disciples had a common purse. They pooled their resources as an indication of their unity with and concern for one another. Others contributed to this purse also, notably the women whom Jesus had healed.

They used the money not only for their daily needs but for giving to the poor. Having a common purse symbolized the transformed relationships characteristic of the redeemed community. Of course, these relationships were not perfect; Judas's hand in the till gives us evidence of that and reminds us that the most benevolent causes can be infiltrated by human greed, at the loss of true *splanchna,* compassion.

## COMPASSION IN THE EARLY CHURCH

Compassionate sharing of food was a hallmark of the early church. They were "one in mind and heart," and the evidence of this was in their willingness to share everything they had and claim nothing as their own (Acts 4:32, TEV). They had communal fellowship meals, "eating with glad and humble hearts," and it was the testimony of this beautiful, loving faith that attracted many to their fellowship. The book of Acts gives many evidences of this sharing, which resulted in no one being in need. Imagine! A community so committed to each other that *no one* was in need. They dared to experiment with a concrete, visible expression of oneness in Christ. Private ownership lost its meaning.

Paul broadened this sharing within the congregation to a sense of responsibility between churches. The collection gathered from the Macedonian churches to aid the church in Jerusalem in its ministry to the poor was an example of this.

This kind of compassionate sharing led to a deeper level of bonding. It is interesting that Paul chose a food metaphor to express the new, close relationship among believers: "Because there is one bread, we who are many are one body, for we all partake of the one bread" (1 Cor. 10:17).

## FOOD AS AN EXPRESSION OF FAITH

The culminating expression of the New Testament understanding of the compassionate use of food is found in James 2:17, where faith is described as dead if not expressed in works. It is the sharing of food and clothing with others that keeps our words of faith from being dead and lifeless. It does no good to say, " 'Go in peace, be warmed and filled,' without giving them the things needed for the body" (v. 16).

Paul's anger over the Corinthians' misuse of the Lord's Supper was based on a similar conviction. It seems that some of the wealthier Corinthians had used the Lord's Supper as an occasion for feasting while poor believers went hungry. Paul felt that this made a mockery of the Eucharist. For him, "discerning the body of Christ" was impossible if one ignored the hungry. Ron Sider puts it vividly: "As long as any Christian anywhere in the world is hungry, the eucharistic celebration of all Christians everywhere in the world is imperfect."[6]

In the New Testament, food is clearly a symbol of the oneness believers find in Christ. It is a gift from God to be enjoyed and freely shared with those who hunger. The promise of the New Testament is that when this attitude prevails, world hunger will cease to exist.

"God is able to provide you with every blessing in abundance, so that you may always have enough of everything and may provide in abundance for every good work" (2 Cor. 9:8).

## FOOD FOR THOUGHT

In the fourth century, one of the early church fathers, Basil the Great, wrote these thought-provoking words:

When someone steals a man's clothes
we call him a thief.
Should we not give the same name
to one who could
clothe the naked
and does not?
The bread in your cupboard
belongs to the hungry man;
the coat hanging unused
in your closet
belongs to the man
who has no shoes;
the money which you
hoard up
belongs to the poor.[7]

Compassion is easy when a specific case is set before us: a sick neighbor to whom we can take a pot of soup or a highly publicized campaign to help starving Ethiopians. The hard part is in "keeping on keeping on." The chaplain in Christopher Fry's play *The Lady's Not for Burning* remarks that it is easy to lose sight of eternal things in the diversity of "the passing moment." This is how it is for most of us. Just as our hospitality gets crowded into corners, our compassion gets swept under the rug. We turn off the TV when another World Vision hunger program comes on the air. It's hard not to feel overwhelmed by the enormity of the global hunger problem; the sight of those swollen bellies and emaciated limbs is almost too much to bear. Besides, what can one individual do? So many stories about so much distress create in us a pall of discouragement.

And then there are the questions: Don't I have a right to the food I have earned? Does my bread really belong to the hungry person who may have done nothing to deserve it? This is the twentieth, not the first century. History has proven that communism doesn't work; are we really supposed to share everything? All these are variations of the question asked of Jesus: "Who is my neighbor?"

If we are to take compassionate food-sharing seriously, we will realize it is an issue not only of love but of justice. Indeed, the two cannot be separated. It is not enough for us to make an annual contribution to a hunger offering or take Meals on Wheels to shut-ins, although these are important. We must also not lose sight of our role in the big picture. We must not give way to discouragement because world hunger is such an enormous problem. Our contribution is real; it is important. Added to the efforts of others like ourselves who refuse to become disheartened, it can change things. There are organizations and agencies that can help us. They do the groundwork: ascertaining need, exploring legislation that can help alleviate hunger, providing support networks on a national and international basis. Does this sound political? It is. Our political system provides a place where our voices can be heard, where our votes count, where our letters to legislators are read.

Solutions for world hunger will come primarily through economic and political change, and we have a role in bringing that about.

RECIPES FOR ACTION

1. Write to these helpful organizations for information about hunger issues:

Bread for the World, 32 Union Square East, New York, NY 10003 (212-260-7000)

Interreligious Task Force on U.S. Food Policy, 110 Maryland Avenue, N.E., Washington, DC 20002

2. Organize a CROP (Community Hunger Appeal of Church World Service) Walk for the Hungry. Write for the guidance manual from: National CROP Office, P.O. Box 968, Elkhart, IN 46515.

3. Keep alert to specific instances where you can share food in a compassionate way: taking a hot meal to an invalid or elderly person, preparing food at a soup kitchen or homeless shelter, contributing to your church's hunger offerings.

4. Should we feel guilty about having so much when two thirds of the world goes to bed hungry every night? Doris Longacre says yes! But after accepting our guilt, the next step is repentance and change. If it is true that we have grown callous to the needs of others, what steps can we take to change? What can we do about exploitation and greed? How can we become more compassionate? Write down three actions you could take.

5. Hand in hand with compassionate sharing goes what Art Fields of Koinonia Partners calls "compassionate living." It is sometimes hard for us to see how our lifestyles affect world hunger. But when two thirds of the world's people go to bed hungry every night, something is off balance. How can we simplify our living so that the imbalance can be adjusted? Doris Longacre's wonderful book *Living More with Less* is a practical handbook of suggestions. Why not read through this book with a group of friends and covenant together to follow some of its suggestions?

# 6 CELEBRATION

## *The Joyful Feast*

Better is a dinner of herbs where love is than a fatted ox and hatred with it.
—Proverbs 15:17

Properly considered, the quality of the dinner is twice blest: it blesses him that gives and him that takes; a dinner with friendliness is the best of all satisfactory meetings—a pompous entertainment, where no love is, is the least satisfactory.
—*Punch*, July 1849

The ultimate aim of civility and good manners is to please: to please one's guest or to please one's host. To this end one uses the rules laid down by tradition: of welcome, generosity, affability, cheerfulness, and consideration for others. People entertain warmly and joyously. To persuade a friend to stay for lunch is a triumph and a precious honour. To entertain many together is to honour them all mutually. It is equally an honour to be a guest.
—Claudia Roden, *A Book of Middle Eastern Food*

Go, eat your bread with enjoyment, and drink your wine with a merry heart; for God has already approved what you do.
—Ecclesiastes 9:7

In the light of all that has been said about the importance of food in bonding rituals, it is no wonder that eating has become an important part of our lives' major celebrations: wedding feasts, birthdays and anniversaries, going-away parties, welcome-home parties, Thanksgiving, Christmas, Easter. If we celebrate, we eat. Birthday cakes, wedding champagne, Fourth of July barbecues—all are symbolic ways of celebrating mutual joy. We mark the significant moments of our lives with knife and fork.

This is nothing new. Our cave-dwelling ancestors undoubtedly celebrated the victorious hunt by sharing the spoils in a joyous feast. Civilizations have developed fine and distinctive cuisines that reach their ultimate glory in the marvelous and complex dishes served up at feasts and banquets. Banquet menus, whether ancient or modern, make a fascinating read. In Jesus' day, the Romans gorged on Minced Nightingales in Vine Leaves and Whole Suckling Pigs Stuffed with Black Puddings. Mark Twain's Christmas dinner included Champignons Flambé, Sweetbreads in Port Wine Sauce, and Sweet Mince Cake, as well as turkey and pheasant. Today, fancy restaurants offer Christmas brunches (which are, in reality, early morning banquets) offering Gallantine of Chicken and Veal, Peach Pancakes Oscar, and Eggnog-Cinnamon Mousse.

In passages like the one from Ecclesiastes, which urges us to eat with enjoyment, it is clear that in the Old Testament eating is seen as a way to express joy in life's most important moments. Feasting affirms the goodness of God's special gift of food and drink. Like all special gifts, however, food and drink can be abused and misused. Banquets can become orgies; feasts can be the source of frustration and fatigue; celebrating can be an excuse for gluttony and drunkenness. The Wisdom literature of the Old Testament contains many warnings against the dangers of surfeit, such as, "Don't associate with people who drink too much or stuff themselves with food. Drunkards and gluttons will be reduced to poverty" (Prov. 23:20–21, TEV). The orgy accompanying the worship of the golden calf in the early history of the exodus became a symbol of the wrong use of feasting where "the people sat down to eat and drink, and rose up to play" with disastrous results (Ex. 32:6).

Although the common people had a very simple daily diet, there were occasions of rich feasting as well. In the chapter on hospitality, we saw how the arrival of a guest was the occasion for a feast, or at least for the best the host could provide. The banquet tables of the kings provided particularly lavish examples of this hospitality. The list in chapter 1 of the supplies Solomon needed each day for his table give us an idea (1 Kings 4:22–23); no wonder the Queen of Sheba was impressed.

Feasting was also used in an intentional way as an instrument for bonding. The Jews were very fond of feasts and banquets. They felt there was nothing better for strengthening the ties of family or the sense of community. Weddings and circumcisions, those special occasions in the life of a family, were always celebrated with lavish food and drink and, with music and dancing, lasted for five or six hours.

## THE ANCIENT FEASTS OF ISRAEL

In addition to its role in hospitality and bonding, feasting played another important part in the life of Israel. It became a primary way to express covenant renewal, as the people sat at table with God to reaffirm the bonds of obligation and kinship. As we look at the most important of the annual celebrations, called the pilgrim festivals, we will see how they helped shape the identity of the new nation and how they continued to influence that nation in New Testament times.

### The Feasts of Passover and Unleavened Bread

The feasts of the Passover and of Unleavened Bread commemorated the beginning of the history of Israel, with the liberation from Egypt and the arrival in the Promised Land. The most important of the annual celebrations in the Old Testament was the Passover, and it continues so today as the feast that reminds

Breaking Bread

the Jewish people of their history and identity. It occurred on the fourteenth day of the month Nisan (or Aviv), which is roughly equivalent to March-April in our calendar. The books of Exodus, Leviticus, and Numbers speak of two feasts, Passover and Unleavened Bread, which were eventually combined into one. The Passover was originally a family ritual and the Feast of Unleavened Bread a community celebration.

The Feast of Unleavened Bread began as an agricultural feast, marked by the first offering of the firstfruits. It was not as old as the Passover feast and was probably not begun until the Israelites had settled in Canaan. It was a preparation for the real harvest festival, the Feast of Weeks, which came at the end of harvest time, while the Feast of Unleavened Bread came at the beginning.

To celebrate the Passover, each family had to offer as sacrifice an unblemished one-year-old male lamb. This lamb was killed at twilight on the fourteenth and its blood sprinkled over the lintel and doorposts of the house. Then the meat was roasted and eaten. No bones of the lamb were to be broken, and the leftovers had to be burned. Unleavened bread and bitter herbs were also a part of the meal, which was, of course, an enactment of the departure from Egypt.

When the two feasts were combined, the Passover was celebrated on the first day of the Feast of Unleavened Bread. The sacrifice was performed in the local sanctuary by the priest. The family then took the lamb, which had been ritually slain, and feasted on it at home. Later, during Josiah's reform, great emphasis was laid on celebrating the Passover in Jerusalem. This meant the ritual sacrifice was done at the Temple, but rented accommodations had to be found for the feast. This gathering of people from all over the country contributed to the Passover's becoming the most important national festival for the Jews.

### The Feast of Weeks

This one-day pilgrimage festival was also called the Harvest Feast or the Day of Firstfruits. To Greek-speaking Jews it became known as Pentecost, because it fell fifty days after the offering of the firstfruits of grain immediately after the celebration of the Passover. Like the Passover, it was originally celebrated in the local sanctuaries until Josiah's reforms, when it was expected that everyone make a pilgrimage to Jerusalem.

The ceremony consisted of offering two loaves made out of the new flour, baked with yeast, which were eaten by the priests. Two lambs were also offered. At the feast of Unleavened Bread, marking the beginning of the harvest, bread without yeast was eaten as a sign of a new beginning; at this feast, marking the end of the harvest, the ordinary leavened bread of the people was eaten as a symbol of the resumption of everyday routines. The cycle of the harvest had come to an end; this feast marked closure.

The Feast of Weeks was a day of solemn joy and thanksgiving for God's protection, which had given a successful harvest. All the men present joined in an altar dance, singing the Hallel. At the end of the day everyone ate in communal meals to which the poor, strangers, and Levites were invited. So this celebrative feast incorporated the rules of hospitality and bonding and became a way for the community to celebrate its unity under God and its obligation to extend hospitality.

Because this feast fell in the third month, it became the feast commemorating the covenant at Sinai, which occurred in the third month after leaving Egypt, according to Exodus 19:1.

The book of Acts records that it was during the Feast of Pentecost that the gift of the Holy Spirit was given, so from that time on, the word "Pentecost" takes on an entirely different significance, signifying the birth of the Christian church.

### The Feast of Booths

The third great annual pilgrim feast was known as Succoth, a Hebrew word that translates literally as "huts" but is commonly known as the Feast of Tabernacles, Booths, or Tents, the Feast of Ingathering, the Feast of the Lord, or simply the Feast. It was the most important and the most popular of the Old Testament pilgrimage feasts.

Like the other two pilgrimage feasts, it was basically an agricultural feast, held when all the produce of the fields had been gathered in, threshed, or pressed.

The hard work of the harvest was completed, and this feast was held in an attitude of joyous festivity and thanksgiving. It was a time of music, dancing, and drinking. Sampling the new wine added to the high-spiritedness of the celebration. In the light of torches, the dancing went on all night to the music of flutes.

At first, there was no fixed day for celebration of this feast, but later it was assigned to the seven days beginning on the fifteenth day of the seventh month, known as Tishri (September–October). It was originally celebrated right in the vineyards or orchards, where small huts, or booths, were built to sleep in. These booths were modeled after the temporary shelters farmers used when they slept in the fields to keep thieves from stealing the ripe fruit. Later, when the feast was held in Jerusalem, these temporary shelters were erected wherever there was space in the city, even on rooftops.

There were several unusual customs in connection with this feast. There was a water libation, in which water from the pool of Siloam was poured on the altar in front of the Temple as a kind of prayer for rain. Everyone carried in one hand a lulab, a kind of ornamental switch made of palm, willow, and myrtle branches, and in the other a citron, which was ceremoniously eaten when the feast was over. These elements, added to the all-night dancing, the feasting and drinking, and the general celebrative, joyous air, contributed to making this the best-loved feast. The saying went, "The man who has never seen the joy of the night of this feast has never seen real joy in all his life."[1]

This feast became connected with the history of the Israelites because, as the book of Leviticus says, the huts reminded them of the temporary shelters the Israelites used in the wilderness (Lev. 23:43).

## FEASTING
## IN THE NEW TESTAMENT

As in the Old Testament, feasting was the way to show hospitality to the stranger and was characterized by the addition of meat to the daily menu. "Killing the fatted calf," as we have seen, entered into common parlance as a symbol for generous hospitality. In New Testament times, if a calf was not available, a kid or lamb was provided. Game, such as deer and gazelle, was popular too. There might also be pigeon, partridge, or quail. And of course there was wine, always red, always filtered, usually diluted with water, sometimes sweetened with honey. Wine was drunk out of large metal goblets or earthenware mugs, which occasioned the many warnings in the book of Proverbs against drunkenness. In Aramaic, the word for wedding was *mishteya'*, a carousing or drinking party. The wedding feast was traditionally served at the house of the groom or his parents, but if he lived a great distance away it was given at the bride's home, and sometimes her parents bore the expense. This was no small matter, for the feasting usually lasted one to two weeks.

The parables give us some idea of the protocol for banquets in New Testament times (see Matt. 22:1–14; Luke 14:7–24). Invitations were delivered by servants. Ceremonial clothing was expected of the guests, usually richly ornamented and colored robes. It was customary for the host, after greeting the guests, to pour perfumed oil on their heads. Guests did not sit or stand, but reclined to eat. When the guests were all in their places, water was brought around for hand washing. Sometimes towels were provided by the host, but sometimes guests brought their own to carry away the gifts that were often given at the end of the meal. The place where one sat was important. The place of honor was at the middle table, where no more than three people sat. Special honor went to the one who sat to the right of the host and "reclined in his bosom." The master served the guests, dipping the bread in the fat or juices of the meat and offering it to the guests as Jesus did to Judas. Eating utensils were almost nonexistent among the common people; the Bible never mentions spoons, and knives only once. Bread served as a fork or spoon, and sometimes as a plate. Sometimes there was a metal plate, because earthenware was considered unclean. Only among the wealthy do we find those things we take for granted: tablecloths, gold or silverplate, knives and spoons. The menus of the wealthy, especially the rulers such as Herod Antipas, were heavily influenced by Roman customs. There were usually three parts: the hors d'oeuvres, accompanied by diluted wine; the three-course dinner itself; and the dessert, consisting of pastries, fresh or dried fruit, and more wine. The excesses of these banquets brought criticisms from the rabbis, who counseled moderation, and perhaps prompted Jesus' question in the Sermon on the Mount: "Is not life more than food?"

Luke 14:1 records a dinner to which Jesus was invited, given by one of the rulers of the Pharisees. It was the custom for the leaders of the synagogue to invite visiting rabbis for dinner on the Sabbath day. The Sabbath did not necessarily mean a frugal repast. Indeed, Plutarch wrote, "The Hebrews honor the Sabbath chiefly by inviting each other to drinking and intoxication." The story is told of a rabbi who bought meat from thirteen butchers that he might be sure to have the best, and paid them at the gate to hurry up the dinner, "and all this in honor of the banquet."

Jesus used the dinner table of the Pharisee on this occasion as a classroom, telling parables that were no doubt inspired by the occasion. The stories dealt with humility and the importance for compassion toward the poor. Perhaps they were triggered by the contrast in the appearance of the man with dropsy, whom Jesus healed, and the opulent meal spread out on the table. The appearance of this man at the table seems somewhat startling to us, but it was not so unusual in New Testament times. Meals like this were often served outside in the courtyard, but even if the meal was inside, it was the custom for spectators to come right inside the house and watch the festivities of the rich.

NEW TESTAMENT
RELIGIOUS FEASTS

In New Testament times, the three pilgrimage festivals were still of central importance to Jewish liturgy, and several other feasts had been added to the Jewish calendar: Yom Kippur, the day of atonement; Hanukkah, commemorating the rededication of the Temple by the Maccabees; and Purim, celebrating the deliverance of the Jewish people from their enemies in the time of Queen Esther.

These feasts never attained the importance of the three pilgrim feasts in the lives of the Jewish people. A part of the reason is that they did not have as a primary purpose the renewal of the covenant bond by sitting "at table" with God, a bond that gave them their identity.

### The Passover

In New Testament times, perhaps as many as a hundred thousand pilgrims came to Jerusalem each year for Passover, which was customarily celebrated in families or with groups of friends. One person was designated to procure the lamb and find a room for the feast (see Jesus' instructions to the disciples in Mark 14:12–15). The sacrifices took place at the Temple, where the priests tossed the blood against the altar as a symbol of declaring the redeeming love of God for the people.

The animals were then returned to the worshipers, who took each one to the quarters rented for the occasion and roasted it in a clay oven. The group of persons celebrating the meal had to number at least ten, but often groups were much larger. Every person had to eat a portion of the sacrificial lamb at least as large as an olive. If the group was very large, other lambs were provided to complete the meal. *The Interpreter's Dictionary of the Bible* gives this description of the meal:

> The meal was served on low tables around which those who partook reclined on cushions, in the manner of a Roman banquet, and all were dressed in festive white. After the blessing the meal opened with a first glass of wine. This was followed by the eating of the lamb with bitter herbs dipped in harosheth, a paste of mashed fruits and nuts. Following a second glass of wine a designated "son" of the family asked the ceremonial question: "Why is this night different from all other nights?" This introduced the recital in song and story of the historical redemption of Israel from slavery in Egypt. It continued with the story of the subsequent crises and deliverances of Israel's long history and ended with a prayer for the redemption of the land from the occupying power of Rome. Following this prayer, which was later changed into a prayer for a return to Jerusalem, the formal commemoration was over. Gatherings could continue informally or members of one group could leave to greet those of another, groups having been kept carefully separate up to this point.[2]

Passover continued to be a pilgrim festival until the destruction of the Temple in A.D. 70. It symbolized freedom and hope to the people, and after the destruction of the Temple it became customary for the supper to close with the words, "Next year in Jerusalem," expressing a hope that never died, that Jerusalem would be restored as a center of Jewish worship.

Was Jesus' meal with the disciples in the upper room a Passover meal? The Synoptic Gospels seem to think it was; John differs, saying the crucifixion occurred on Passover eve. There is no reference to lamb, the word for leavened instead of unleavened bread is used, and only one cup of wine rather than the ritual four is mentioned. But these arguments do not rule out the Passover. The purpose of the Gospel writers was not to describe the Passover ritual in detail but to report those words and acts that became a basis for the ritual observance of the Lord's Supper in the early church.

There are many indications of the Passover in the Synoptics. Mark gives the following:

It was the first day of Unleavened Bread, when the passover lamb was sacrificed (14:12).

The disciples prepared an upper room for the meal (14:15–16).

Jesus dipped bread into a dish (the haroseth that would have accompanied the passover lamb—14:20).

The "cup of blessing" indicated more than an ordinary meal (14:23).

The prayer of thanksgiving offered by Jesus is like that offered by the head of the house at the Passover (14:23).

It seems clear that in Jesus' mind the supper had a significance that went beyond the Passover. It was a symbol of the messianic banquet he would share with his followers in the coming of the kingdom. The messianic banquet was a familiar image in apocalyptic writings. Jesus used it to remind his disciples of that hope: they would receive not only deliverance from the bondage of sin, but joy and gladness in the unity of table where the Lord is host. A feast of fat things. No more tears. No more death. These are the promises from the messianic banquet image that would be renewed each time they "broke bread together."

### The Lord's Supper

For the early church, then, the primary feast was not the Passover but the Lord's Supper or the Eucharist. Two of its purposes were similar to the Passover: remembering and covenant renewal. The Haggadah, the body of work that interprets the obligations of Judaism, says in reference to the Passover, "In every single generation it is a man's duty to regard himself as if he had gone forth from Egypt." The ritual of the Lord's Supper includes the words, "As often as you eat this bread and drink the cup, you proclaim the Lord's death until he come" (1 Cor. 11:26). In addition to these two purposes, there is a third expressed in this passage: the anticipation of life in the age to come.

The early church seems to have celebrated the Lord's Supper every day, "day by day . . . breaking bread . . . with glad and generous hearts" (Acts 2:46). Their joy over the resurrection coupled with their excitement over being part of a special company made their shared meals a happy anticipation of things to come. A part of that anticipation was of the immediate coming of Christ. Perhaps the fact that many of Christ's resurrection appearances occurred during meals spurred them to believe he would return while they were breaking bread together. But as time went on and his immediate return did not occur, and as the church spread outside Jerusalem, it became more and more difficult to sustain this daily shared meal. Before the end of the apostolic period, this regular gathering of Christians was relegated to the first day of the week. Acts 20:7 speaks of gathering together to "break bread" on the first day of the week, which became known to Christians as the Lord's Day. Central to the worship on this day was the supper, known from the second century on as the Eucharist.

The Lord's Supper is easily identifiable as a feast that contains the elements of gratitude for God's good gifts, hospitality (as we are guests at the Lord's table), bonding (we are one body for we partake of one bread), and celebration. It is not so easy to connect it with the theme of compassion. Joseph Grassi's stimulating work *Broken Bread and Broken Bodies* effectively makes that connection. He points out reference after reference in the New Testament where the connection is made between the Eucharist and food-sharing. Paul's warning about self-examination before partaking of the Eucharist, he says, is given because a special sign of members of the body of Christ is love and concern for those who are suffering and in need.[3] Just as the Passover was a renewal of covenant commitment, so the Eucharist calls us to renew our commitment to the one whose ministry was to the poor, the needy, the hungry, the oppressed.

FOOD FOR THOUGHT

One of the most well-known feasts in literature is the Cratchits' Christmas dinner. Here's how Charles Dickens described it:

> There never was such a goose. Bob said he didn't believe there ever was such a goose cooked. Its tenderness and flavor, size and cheapness, were the themes of universal admiration. Eked out by apple-sauce and mashed potatoes, it was a sufficient dinner for the whole family; indeed, as Mrs. Cratchit said with great delight (surveying one small atom of a bone upon the dish), they hadn't ate it all at last! Yet everyone had had enough. . . . There was nothing of high mark in this. They were not a handsome family; they were not well dressed; their shoes were far from being waterproof . . . but they were happy, grateful, pleased with one another, and contented with the time.

These words echo not only Proverbs, "Better a dinner of herbs where love is . . ." but the verse from Acts describing the early Christians who "partook of food with glad and generous hearts." The poignancy of the Cratchits' "feast" creates in us a wistful longing that all our tables might reflect that glow. There's no mention here of gluttony, or exhaustion, or boredom, or dissatisfaction with the menu from those around the table.

In the biblical understanding, festal celebrations are to be joyous, playful reminders of who we are, opportunities for expressing gratitude for God's abundant love, and symbolic reenactments of the harmonious gathering to come around the Lord's kingdom table. Father Robert Capon puts it in a slightly different way: "Food is the daily sacrament of unnecessary goodness, ordained for a continual remembrance that the world will always be more delicious than it is useful."[4]

### RECIPES FOR ACTION

1. Think for a moment about the great feast of the Christian community, Holy Communion. What attitudes do you bring to it? Is it a joyful feast or a solemn remembering? Do you recognize Christ as your host when you sit at the table? Do you feel like a guest or an estranged spectator?

The next time you take Communion, let your five senses draw you into the wholeness of the experience. What do you hear? What do you see? What do you smell? What do you taste? What words do you say?

2. Thanksgiving and Christmas are religious feasts that have tended to become ceremonies of gluttony in our American culture and have thereby lost much of their original meaning in the frantic preparation of more food than anyone can eat. List three things you might do to regain the spirit of a Puritan Thanksgiving and a "Cratchit Christmas" in your home. (Hint: you might start with the word "simplify.")

3. If your church has never had a seder meal on Holy Thursday, volunteer to help plan one.

# 7 HOPE AND RESTORATION

## *No More Tears*

In paradise . . . he will be waited on by three hundred attendants while he eats, and shall be served in dishes of gold, whereof three hundred shall be set before him at once, containing each a different kind of food, the last morsel of which shall be as grateful as the first.

—The Koran

On this mountain the LORD of hosts will make for all peoples a feast of fat things, a feast of wine on the lees, of fat things full of marrow, of wine on the lees well refined.

—Isaiah 25:6

Blessed are those who are invited to the marriage supper of the Lamb.
—Revelation 19:9

Almost every one of us has experienced the healing and restorative power of food. Whether it be warm cookies and milk, or a good cup of tea, or hearty stew on a bitterly cold day, food has the power to renew us, restore our energy, and give us hope to face what lies ahead.

## THE MESSIANIC BANQUET

It is not surprising, then, that the culminating image of food in biblical understanding is the messianic banquet. It combines the elements of hospitality, bonding, compassion, and celebration to symbolize the hope and restoration awaiting the people of God in the consummation of the kingdom. It was an image used frequently in the apocryphal writings, where it represented fellowship with God in the last days. In the apocryphal book of the Ethiopian Enoch, chapter 62:14, we find these words: "The Lord God will dwell over them, and they will eat and lie down and rise up to all eternity with that Son of Man." The guests at this banquet are the righteous and the elect. In another book from the Apocrypha, the Slavic Enoch 42:5, there is this description: "Joyously awaiting his feast, the enjoyment of good things, of immeasurable wealth and joy and happiness in light and everlasting life." Third Enoch 48:10 tells that Israel is to enjoy a banquet in Jerusalem with the Messiah. The Apocalypse of Elijah speaks of the messianic age between this age and the age to come when the righteous are to rejoice and eat with the Messiah. During this period, food will be abundant, trees will be loaded with fruit, and wheat, wine, and oil will reproduce themselves nine-hundred-fold. By the time of Christ, a common expression of the anticipation of this banquet was, "Blessed is he who shall eat bread in the kingdom of God!" We have already observed that when this was piously invoked at the Pharisee's table (Luke 14:15), Jesus responded with a parable, giving a different picture of the eucharistic banquet, which suggested that there might be some surprises in store.

The image of a final banquet that included both rejoicing and judgment was an important part of the eschatology of Israel. Judgment is clearly the bottom line of the passage in Zephaniah 1:7, which describes a sacrifice or feast on the Day of the Lord to which the Lord has invited guests. The guests, however, are the enemies of Israel, and the sacrificial victim is Israel herself. Not exactly an image of peaceful and joyous reconciliation!

## THE BIG PICNIC
## ON THE MOUNTAIN

For an eschatological feast that celebrates reconciliation, we must turn again to Isaiah 25:6–9. The occasion is a pilgrimage to God's holy place, Mount Zion, but this time the pilgrims are not just the Israelites but "all peoples." Usually when other nations were described as coming to Zion, it was to pay tribute to God as a powerful monarch, as we see in Psalm 68:29: "Because of thy temple at Jerusalem kings bear gifts to thee." There are also descriptions of the services that will be provided by foreign peoples, such as taking care of the Israelites' flocks and fields and vineyards (see Isa. 61:5). In Isaiah 25, however, there is a new eschatological vision. Instead of just bringing tribute, the other nations will have a share in the feast as well. The event is a coronation feast celebrating God's rule throughout the whole world. By recognizing God as king and by participating in table fellowship, all nations are brought into fellowship with God and with one another. There is no Berlin Wall in the kingdom, no apartheid. Luke echoes this in two places: when the angel announces good news of great joy which will come to "all the people" (2:10) and in the thirteenth chapter's description of the eschatological banquet when people shall come "from east and west, and from north and south, and sit at table in the kingdom of God" (v. 29). God as host extends hospitality without question to the stranger. The promise in Psalm 22:27 will be fulfilled: "All the ends of the earth shall remember and turn to the LORD; and all the families of the nations shall worship before him."

What is the menu for this picnic to end all picnics? There will be "fat things" and "wine on the lees." In a land where meat was scarce, fat was highly treasured, especially the marrow in the bones. It is like saying, "There will be filet mignon and apple pie à la mode." Wine on the lees simply means aged wine that has acquired full flavor from the dregs, or "lees," and then been poured off, clarified. It was the best.

The people will come to the feast still covered with mourning for all the suffering they have endured. The Lord will tear the veils from their faces and, seeing the tears on their cheeks, will gently wipe them away. And these are the last tears they will shed, for death will be destroyed forever. This is one of the tenderest pictures of God in all of scripture. It finds an echo in Revelation 21:4: "He will wipe away every tear from their eyes, and death shall be no more, neither shall there be mourning nor crying nor pain any more."

It is hard for us to imagine how radical this passage was in the time of Isaiah. Not only are the foreign nations to be permitted to attend the banquet, but death is to be literally swallowed up. So little is said in the Old Testament about the afterlife that this is amazing. Who could have hoped for this? And then there is the dramatic picture of the Ruler of the universe stooping down tenderly to wipe the tears from the faces of the people, a trivial act of service that shows clearly God's great love for all people.

Finally, shame and disgrace will be removed. To the Jews, this probably meant that they would be vindicated; they would suffer no more jibes of "Where is your God?" because all would see the glory of God. They would no longer have to live with the contradiction of being the people of God yet subject to the Gentiles. They would be free from reproach and shame, free to be who they really were: God's own people. This is a picture of a day of redemption, a day of restoration.

And what will be the response of the people, those starving multitudes, to this great feast, this feast filled with good things: life everlasting, hope and restoration, freedom from tears, freedom from guilt and shame? They will shout aloud, "Lo, this is our God; we have waited for him, that he might save us. This is the LORD; we have waited for him; let us be glad and rejoice in his salvation" (v.9). Their hope in God will not be disappointed. God will be in their midst; doubts give way to assurance. God will bring deliverance and restoration as they gather around the table.

THE BANQUET PARABLES

Jesus' parables used images and situations drawn from everyday life that, on the surface, appear simple and obvious. However, both he and his hearers were aware of nuances lost to us in the layers of symbolic meaning attached to many of these commonplace occurrences. For instance, in the symbolic language of the East, the wedding is the symbol of the day of salvation. The banquet, also, was an expression of the final reconciliation between God and human beings, as we saw so beautifully expressed in the Isaiah 25 passage. Jesus used both wedding and banquet images in his teachings about the kingdom, and these are especially vivid in the parables.

### The Place of Honor Parable
### (Luke 14:1–14)

Although some biblical scholars hesitate to call this passage a true parable, it does have the primary qualifications of a parable; it uses a familiar situation of daily life to make a point. On the surface, it sounds like a restatement of rules for social etiquette long familiar to the Jews. There is a strong similarity to the verses in Proverbs 25:6–7: "Do not put yourself forward in the king's presence or stand in the place of the great; for it is better to be told, 'Come up here,' than to be put lower in the presence of the prince."

However, Jesus takes these rules and interprets them in a way that moves them several notches above Amy Vanderbilt's advice about table manners. He had been observing the expressions on the faces of the Pharisees at a Sabbath dinner party: the calculating way they watched him, their disgust when the man swollen with dropsy entered the room, their chagrin as Jesus asked them a Catch-22 question about the Law, and, finally, the air of superiority with which they vied for places of honor at the head table.

As they settled into their reclining positions around the table, Jesus began to talk quietly about the rules of etiquette. And then he suddenly shifted emphasis. His lesson on decency and order became a picture of the kingdom way of doing things. The contrast in this way and the way the Pharisees did things could not have been missed by the most dense observer. The Pharisees had elevated separateness into a religious principle: they refused to associate with those who did not keep the Law. And since theirs was a religion of merit where rewards are given based on scrupulous observance of the Law, it is not surprising that reciprocity characterized their dealings with each other as well. "You scratch my back, I'll scratch yours" made sense to them.

In just a few graphic words, Jesus turned that notion of separateness upside down. Don't invite those who will "invite you back"; invite society's outcasts instead, and you will be rewarded on the day of resurrection because you have understood the spirit and purpose of God.

This was not a message the Pharisees wanted to hear. Nor is it a message we care to hear today. We prefer our stratified societies, our caste systems, our separateness, of which one of the most starkly dramatic examples is the chasm created in South Africa by the destructiveness of apartheid. What Jesus is talking about in this parable is the love that bridges that chasm.

There is no better illustration of this love than a passage in Alan Paton's story *Ah, but Your Land Is Beautiful.* The setting is a black African church, the occasion a foot-washing ceremony. One by one, the pastor, Mr. Buti, had called the people to come forward to take part in the ceremony, either washing another's feet or having their own feet washed. Then he called the name of Martha Fortuin.

> So Martha Fortuin, who thirty years earlier had gone to work in the home of the newly married Advocate Olivier of Bloemfontein, and had gone with him to Cape Town and Pretoria when he became a judge, and had returned with him to Bloemfontein when he became a justice of the Appellate Court, now left her seat to walk to the chair before the altar. She walked with head downcast as becomes a modest and devout woman, conscious of the honor that had been done her by the Reverend Isaiah Buti. Then she heard him call out the name of Jan Christian Olivier and, though she was herself silent, she heard the gasp of the congregation as the great judge of Bloemfontein walked up to the altar to wash her feet.
> Then Mr. Buti gave the towel to the judge and the judge, as the word says, girded himself with it, and took the dish of water, and knelt at the feet of Martha Fortuin. He took her right foot in his hands and washed it and dried it with the towel. Then he took her other foot in his hands and washed it and dried it with the towel. Then he took both her feet in his hands with gentleness, for they were no doubt tired with much serving, and he kissed them both. Then Martha

Fortuin, and many others in the Holy Church of Zion, fell a-weeping in that holy place.[1]

The banquet table of our Lord is a place of true community, where the world's values are set aside and genuine harmony prevails.

It is indeed a difficult message to hear. Even James and John, those most beloved disciples, wanted a promise from Jesus that they would have places of honor at the eschatological banquet. Once more Jesus had to remind them that true greatness is found in the humility of the servant role (see Mark 10:35–45).

*The Great Banquet Parable*
*(Matthew 22:1–10; Luke 14:15–24)*

As Jesus finished telling the place of honor parable, the mention of resurrection triggered an automatic reaction from one guest, who chimed out with a pious slogan associated with anticipation of the eschatological banquet: "Blessed is he who shall eat bread in the kingdom of God!"

Once more, Jesus turned the conversation around. "Do you really want to go to that banquet?" he seems to be asking. "Or have you just ignored the RSVP on the invitation? It's not enough to be invited; you have to accept." Jesus was well aware that the Pharisees had opted for hiding behind a religious system rather than for responding to the gracious, freeing good news he had offered them. They had refused to hear his invitation to a new understanding of the kingdom, one based on love and compassion rather than on self-righteousness.

The Matthew and Luke versions of this parable are very different. Matthew's is more of an allegory, dealing with the rejection of Jesus. Luke's version is a true parable and may be recorded exactly as Jesus spoke it. It has been suggested that, in Luke's parable, Jesus is saying that persons are excluded from the kingdom only by their own choice. The excuses given in Luke's version were valid reasons for letting a man off military duty in that day, but they are not valid reasons to ignore God's call. Those who let earthly preoccupations, including legalistic piety, become more attractive than sitting at table with God, lose the kingdom.

The parable also says something about the kind of people who were eagerly responding to the good news Jesus is offering. They are the underdogs of the Jewish population: the *'am ha'aretz*, the people of the land, who in their struggle to survive no longer care the least bit about the law. They were despised by the Pharisees, who must have therefore found this parable particularly objectionable.

Frederick Buechner has a fascinating contemporary version of this parable in his novel *The Love Feast*. The story's unlikely hero, Leo Bebb, wants to do something generous for the college students in Boston, so he plans a magnificent Thanksgiving dinner . . . and no one comes. Bebb does what the host of the parable does; he sends his friends out into the streets to invite anyone they find to the feast. It is a great success. The strangers gathered up in this fashion—nuns, the homeless, lonely older people, and even a number of college students—begin to talk to one another, and, under the mellowing influence of good food and wine, barriers drop away. Bebb is so thrilled by the success of his party, so "drunk on the occasion," that he begins to speak to the group "in such a disconnected way that you had to listen if only to hear what he was going to bounce to next." He said:

> The kingdom of heaven is like a great feast. That's the way of it. The kingdom of heaven is a love feast where nobody's a stranger. Like right here. There's strangers everywhere else you can think of. There's strangers was born twin brothers out of the same womb. There's strangers was raised together in the same town and worked side by side all their life through. There's strangers got married and been climbing in and out of the same four-poster thirty-five, forty years and they're strangers still. And Jesus, it's like most of the time he is a stranger, too. But here in this place there's no strangers, and Jesus, he isn't a stranger either. The Kingdom of Heaven's like this.[2]

The parable of the great banquet makes three points: (1) no one can enter the kingdom without God's invitation; (2) no one can remain outside but by his or her deliberate choice; and (3) since we are not the ones who choose the other guests, we may be in for some surprises. This last point is also made by Matthew in the story of the healing of the centurion's servant. Jesus' words indicate that not only will there be some surprising guests at the great banquet who will come "from east and west," but, even more shockingly, they hint that Israel may herself end up excluded from the warmth of the banquet hall and weeping in the darkness outside by her own deliberate choice (see Matt. 8:11–12). Here the familiar eschatological vision of Gentile kings paying homage to Jerusalem is altered to picture Gentiles coming to the New Jerusalem "to sit at table with Abraham, Isaac, and Jacob," a table at which Jesus himself will be the host. Although Luke places these words of Jesus in a different context, in answer to the question about how many will enter the kingdom, the warning is the same. Those who have thought they would have places of honor at the messianic feast will find themselves thrust out, and those same surprising Gentile guests from the four corners of the earth will occupy the places of honor.

### THE LAST SUPPER

There can be no question but that the Last Supper was in Jesus' mind an anticipation of the messianic banquet he would share with his disciples in the coming kingdom. He doubtless had in mind the imagery of the banquet as a symbol of the life of the age to come.

For Christians, the Supper is a symbol of the final consummation of God's redemptive purpose, whether viewed as already accomplished in the death and resurrection of Jesus, or as yet to come in the eschatological banquet at the end of time. The Supper, therefore, witnesses to a kingdom that is paradoxically both here and now and also yet to come. It offers a message of present hope and future restoration to all who partake of it.

The early Christians imitated the Last Supper with their agape meals, shared feasts of communal love. At first, there was not a clear distinction between the agape and the Eucharist, but by the middle of the second century the two celebrations were quite distinct. At the agape, the procedure seems to have been to follow the guest-meal ritual described in chapter 3.

These agape meals had several purposes. The first was simply fellowship:

they served to strengthen the bonds of the community. This became increasingly important as the church experienced persecution. Second, the suppers provided opportunities for showing compassion to the poor and to widows. Third, they kept alive the message of hope through the preaching, prophesying, and singing of "psalms and hymns and spiritual songs" that accompanied them (Col. 3:16). These suppers were constant reminders of the great banquet to come, when all things would be restored to their rightful order and all people united in shalom.

### THE MARRIAGE FEAST
### OF THE LAMB

The culminating image of hope and resurrection, however, is the blending of wedding feast and eschatological banquet that we find in the Revelation of John. In Revelation 3:20, Jesus promises to share a meal with prospective martyrs, symbolizing the final and complete bonding and acceptance that will be theirs. The rhythmic beauty of the poetry expresses the mutuality and unity to be experienced at the table: "I will come in to him and eat with him, and he with me."

The metaphor gets a bit confused in 19:7–9, where the guests are also the bride of the Lamb, but the symbol once again is one of a joyful unity with Christ, a complete bonding, a recognition of the kinship around a banquet table that celebrates the coming together of heaven and earth and the completion of God's great design.

We have been given foretastes of this banquet—the family table, a cup of tea with a dear friend, bread-making, Christmas feasts—and the foretastes make us hungry for the fullness of the banquet that is yet to come. Robert Capon, in his remarkable theological cookbook *The Supper of the Lamb*, describes this longing poignantly:

> All tastes fade, of course but not the taste for greatness they inspire; each love escapes us, but not the longing it provokes for a better "convivium," a

higher session. We embrace the world in all its glorious solidity, yet it struggles in our very arms, declares itself a pilgrim world, and, through the lattices and windows of its nature, discloses cities more desirable still. . . . For all its rooted loveliness, the world has no continuing city here; it is an outlandish place, a foreign home, a session in via to a better version of itself—and it is our glory to see it so and thirst until Jerusalem comes home at last.[3]

The wedding feast of the Lamb is the ultimate Thanksgiving dinner, where the promises made in Isaiah 25 are finally realized: no more mourning, or crying, or pain, or death. It is a glorious family reunion, when God and God's people will be brought together, reconciled wholly and completely. It is a New Year's Eve party, the dawn of a new age, when, as Julian of Norwich expressed it, "All shall be well, and all shall be well, and all manner of thing shall be well." It will be a feast to end all feasts, one that satisfies our deepest hungers and thirsts. When we sit at that table, receiving the loving hospitality of our Lord, we will know that we belong, that we are bonded in a covenant even stronger than the covenant of salt, to a God who loves us, who celebrates with us, and who gives us hope of restoration and peace.

> "Let us rejoice and exult and give him the glory,
> for the marriage of the Lamb has come,
> and his Bride has made herself ready;
> It was granted her to be clothed with fine linen, bright and pure"—
> for the fine linen is the righteous deeds of the saints.
> And the angel said to me, "Write this:
> Blessed are those who are invited to the marriage supper of the Lamb."
> Revelation 19:7–9

FOOD FOR THOUGHT

Karen Burton Mains has written a thoughtful book on Christian hospitality, *Open Heart—Open Home*. She closes the book with a prayer from which I have excerpted the following petitions:

Lord,
Thank you for having given Yourself in intimate,
inexplicable hospitality.
You have been the Host to all creation.

Without meat You have nourished us.
Without beverage You have refreshed us.
By Your very Word came sustenance.
On bread and water without price have we been fed.
You have been manna in the wilderness of our lives.

Without a table You have banqueted us,
inviting us, yea, to be married unto You.
Over our heads flies the banner of Your love.
We are entertained with the mysteries of faith,
the songs of the Spirit, holy laughter.
You have garmented us in festal righteousness. . . .

You are the Host of all . . .
Lifted up, suffering, without breath, You yet
extend greeting to all the masses,
"Come unto me . . .
come . . .
come . . .

You give us the mystery of Your presence
in this supper of the ages, this remembrance of
Your ultimate hospitality.

O Lord,
Make my hospitality as unto Yours.
Be forever my archetype of endeavor,
My firstfruit of harvested goodness:
Love for the battered, misused child,
Grace to bind running ulcers of flesh and soul,
Eagerness for the wealthy without servility,
And for the poor without superiority.

Through eternity You have been and will be
utterly hospitable.
Help me,
poor, faltering, unfeeling me,
to be like You,
with breath-beat and soul-heart
poured out
emptied
opened.
Help me,
to be given to hospitality."[4]

The invitation to the banquet has been given. "The Spirit and the Bride say, 'Come.' And let the one who hears say, 'Come.' And let the one who is thirsty come, let the one who desires take the water of life without price" (Rev. 22:17, RSV alt.)

RECIPES FOR ACTION

1.  Close your eyes and imagine that you are sitting at the banquet table in the New Jerusalem. What hungers do you have that will be filled there? Take a few minutes to list your deepest needs. Now look at your list. What can you do now to begin to appease these hungers? Are there people who could help? Books you could read? Is there a way to restructure your lifestyle so that your hungers can be met? Jot down some things you could do, and choose one on which to begin to focus now.

2.  What does chapter 5 on compassion have to do with this chapter? Is there a connection between feeding others and being fed? Between giving hope to others and having hope yourself? Think about it.

# NOTES

---

*Full publication information, when not given, may be found in the Bibliography.*

## 1. BIBLICAL FOODS AND CUSTOMS

1. *The Interpreter's Dictionary of the Bible,* vol. 2, p. 261.
2. Ibid., p. 323.
3. Ibid., p. 306.
4. André L. Simon, *A Concise Encyclopaedia of Gastronomy* (London, 1939), quoted in Stella Standard, *Our Daily Bread,* p. vii.

## 2. STEWARDSHIP: FOOD AS GOD'S GOOD GIFT

1. Walter Brueggemann, *Genesis,* p. 39.
2. Søren Kierkegaard, quoted in Vernard Eller, *The Simple Life* (Grand Rapids: Wm. B. Eerdmans Publishing Co., 1973), pp. 28–29.
3. Douglas John Hall, *Imaging God,* p. 52.
4. Joseph Addison, quoted in *Consuming Passions,* ed. by Jonathon Green, p. 277.
5. John Calvin, *Commentary on the First Epistle of Paul to the Corinthians,* p. 347.
6. Ibid.
7. André L. Simon, quoted in Stella Standard, *Our Daily Bread,* p. vii.

### 3. HOSPITALITY:
### EXPRESSION OF GRACE

1.  Quoted by William Cruickshank, "Hospitality (Semitic)," in *The Encyclopedia of Religion and Ethics*, ed. by James Hastings, vol. 6, p. 816.
2.  J. B. Mathews, "Hospitality and the New Testament Church," p. 36–45.
3.  John Koenig, *New Testament Hospitality*, p. 2.
4.  Thomas W. Ogletree, *Hospitality to the Stranger*, p. 2.
5.  Parker J. Palmer, *The Company of Strangers*, p. 69.
6.  John Scott, Untitled prayer-poem in *Alive Now*, vol. 18, no. 6, p. 31.
7.  Lynne Hundley, "No More Strangers," p. 13.
8.  Henri Nouwen, *Reaching Out*, pp. 56–58.

### 4. BONDING:
### STRANGERS NO LONGER

1.  Roland de Vaux, *Ancient Israel*, vol. 2, pp. 417–418.
2.  William F. Arndt, *St. Luke*, p. 169.
3.  Joseph Grassi, *Broken Bread and Broken Bodies*, p. 83.
4.  Bernard O'Kelly, ed., *John Colet's Commentary on First Corinthians*, p. 59.
5.  Wendy Wright, "In the Circle of a Mother's Arms," *Weavings*, vol. 3, no. 1, p. 18.
6.  Markus Barth, *Rediscovering the Lord's Supper*, p. 73.
7.  Joseph Grassi, *Broken Bread and Broken Bodies*, p. 62.

### 5. COMPASSION:
### THE GREAT INASMUCH

1.  The poem by Yorifumi Yaguchi of Sapporo, Japan, is quoted in Doris Janzen Longacre, *Living More with Less*, p. 20.
2.  Longacre, *Living More with Less*, p. 246.
3.  Ronald J. Sider, *Rich Christians in an Age of Hunger*, p. 55.
4.  Mother Teresa of Calcutta and Brother Roger of Taizé, *Meditations on the Way of the Cross*.
5.  Sider, *Rich Christians in an Age of Hunger*, p. 69.
6.  Ibid., p. 106.
7.  Longacre, *Living More with Less*, p. 13.

## 6. CELEBRATION:
## THE JOYFUL FEAST

1. Roland de Vaux, *Ancient Israel*, vol. 2, p. 496.
2. J. C. Rylaarsdam, "Passover," *The Interpreter's Dictionary of the Bible*, vol. 3, p. 665.
3. Joseph Grassi, *Broken Bread and Broken Bodies*, p. 86.
4. Robert F. Capon, *The Supper of the Lamb*, p. 40.

## 7. HOPE AND RESTORATION:
## NO MORE TEARS

1. Alan Paton, *Ah, but Your Land Is Beautiful*, pp. 234–235.
2. Frederick Buechner, *Love Feast*, p. 56.
3. Robert F. Capon, *The Supper of the Lamb*, p. 190.
4. Karen Burton Mains, *Open Heart—Open Home*, pp. 197–199.

# BIBLIOGRAPHY

Arndt, William F. *St. Luke*. Classic Commentary series. St. Louis: Concordia Publishing House, 1956.

Barth, Markus. *Rediscovering the Lord's Supper: Communion with Israel, with Christ, and Among the Guests*. Atlanta: John Knox Press, 1988.

Brueggemann, Walter. *Genesis*. Interpretation: The Bible Commentary for Teaching and Preaching. Atlanta: John Knox Press, 1982.

Buechner, Frederick. *Love a Feast*. San Francisco: Harper & Row, 1979.

Calvin, John. *Commentary on the First Epistle of Paul to the Corinthians*. Grand Rapids: Wm. B. Eerdmans Publishing Co., 1948.

Capon, Robert F. *The Supper of the Lamb: A Culinary Reflection*. New York: Harcourt, Brace and Co., 1967.

Cruickshank, William. "Hospitality (Semitic)," in *Encyclopaedia of Religion and Ethics*, ed. by James Hastings, vol. 6. Edinburgh: T. & T. Clark, 1926.

de Vaux, Roland. *Ancient Israel*, vol. 2, *Religious Institutions*. New York: McGraw-Hill Book Co., 1965.

Grabhorn, Robert. *A Commonplace Book of Cookery*. San Francisco: North Point Press, 1985.

Grassi, Joseph. *Broken Bread and Broken Bodies: The Eucharist and World Hunger*. Maryknoll, N.Y.: Orbis Books, 1985.

Green, Jonathon, ed. *Consuming Passions*. New York: Fawcett Columbine, 1985.

Hall, Douglas J. *Imaging God: Dominion as Stewardship*. Grand Rapids: Wm. B. Eerdmans Publishing Co., 1986.

Hundley, Lynn. "No More Strangers," *Alive Now*, vol. 18. Nashville: The Upper Room, 1988.

*The Interpreter's Dictionary of the Bible*. Nashville: Abingdon Press, 1962.

Johnson, Luke T. *Sharing Possessions: Mandate and Symbol of Faith*. Overtures to Biblical Theology. Philadelphia: Fortress Press, 1981.

Koenig, John. *New Testament Hospitality: Partnership with Strangers as Promise and Mission*. Overtures to Biblical Theology. Philadelphia: Fortress Press, 1985.

Longacre, Doris Janzen. *Living More with Less*. Scottdale, Pa.: Herald Press, 1980.

Mains, Karen Burton. *Open Heart—Open Home*. Elgin, Ill.: David C. Cook Publishing Co., 1976.

Mathews, J. B. "Hospitality and the New Testament Church: An Historical and Exegetical Study." Dissertation, Princeton Theological Seminary, 1964.

Mother Teresa of Calcutta and Brother Roger of Taizé. *Meditations on the Way of the Cross*. New York: Pilgrim Press 1987.

Nouwen, Henri J. M. *Reaching Out: The Three Movements of Spiritual Life*. Garden City, N.Y.: Doubleday & Co., 1975.

Ogletree, Thomas W. *Hospitality to the Stranger: Dimensions of Moral Understanding*. Philadelphia: Fortress Press, 1985.

O'Kelly, Bernard, ed. and tr. *John Colet's Commentary on First Corinthians*. Binghamton, N.Y.: Medieval and Renaissance Texts and Studies, 1985.

Palmer, Parker J. *The Company of Strangers: Christians and the Renewal of America's Public Life*. New York: Crossroad Publishing Co., 1986.

Paton, Alan. *Ah, but Your Land Is Beautiful*. New York: Charles Scribner's Sons, 1982.

Scott, John. Untitled prayer-poem in *Alive Now*, vol. 18, no. 6, p. 31. Nashville: The Upper Room, 1988.

Sider, Ronald J. *Rich Christians in an Age of Hunger: A Biblical Study*. Downers Grove, Ill.: Intervarsity Press, 1977.

Simon, Arthur. *Bread for the World*. Rev. ed. New York: Paulist Press, 1985.

Standard, Stella. *Our Daily Bread*. New York: Funk & Wagnalls Co., 1970.

Wright, Wendy. "In the Circle of a Mother's Arms," *Weavings*, vol. 3, no. 1, p. 18. Nashville: The Upper Room, 1988.

# INDEX OF SCRIPTURE REFERENCES

# ACKNOWLEDGMENTS

Unless noted otherwise, scripture quotations are from the Revised Standard Version of the Bible, copyright 1946, 1952, © 1971, 1973 by the Division of Christian Education of the National Council of the Churches of Christ in the U.S.A., and are used by permission.

Scripture quotations marked TEV are from the *Good News Bible—Old Testament:* Copyright © American Bible Society 1976; *New Testament:* Copyright © American Bible Society 1966, 1971, 1976.

Grateful acknowledgment is made to the following for permission to reprint copyrighted material.

Abingdon Press, Nashville, from *The Interpreter's Dictionary of the Bible,* edited by George Arthur Buttrick. Copyright renewal © 1990 Abingdon Press.

David C. Cook Publishing Co., Elgin, Ill., from *Open Heart—Open Home,* by Karen Burton Mains, copyright 1976.

Herald Press, Scottdale, Pa., for poem by Yorifumi Yaguchi and poetic quotation from Basil the Great, in Doris Janzen Longacre, *Living More with Less,* © 1980.

John Scott, for prayer-poem in *Alive Now,* vol. 18, no. 6 (1988), published by The Upper Room, Nashville.